AS THIS BILL SEES IT:

LESSONS LEARNED IN A.A. MEETINGS

BILL E.

Copyright © 2013 Bill E.
All rights reserved.

ISBN: 1482007290
ISBN 13: 978-1482007299

Using multiple sources including personal stories, great literature from the Bible, classical literature, children's stories and recovery literature, the author provides different perspectives on why it makes sense to get and remain sober. The author at times challenges some of the assumptions of the original authors of the Big Book of Alcoholics Anonymous but remains true to the promise made that more will be revealed. The author, like all recovering alcoholics is indebted to Bill Wilson and Bob Smith who without their original thoughts and words, would not have recovered from his own case of helplessness.

Most of these lessons were learned in multiple A.A. meetings over the several years the author has been attending A. A. meetings, mostly in and around Rochester, New York. The lessons came about not only from listening to what many in A. A. call the voice of a higher power but because true, to his profession he believed in taking notes either directly in the meetings or immediately writing them down afterwards. Reflecting on what he heard and read and relating that material made the material valuable to him and hopefully to the reader of this book. The author believes that few of us can only remember what we have only heard in meetings or in the classroom. As the author argues in one of the readings that follow the person who attends meetings is going to do better than those who don't and that the more we are engaged the more likely we are to learn the lessons of the day.

The author, respecting the anonymity of Alcoholics Anonymous uses only his first name. He is a retired college professor, father of two sons and five grandchildren. He has been married at the time of this publication for almost 50 years to a woman he met in first grade. He has been sober since 1988.

AS THIS BILL SEES IT

JANUARY 1

Police reports on the claims of drivers stopped for DWI or involved in a car accident indicate that the number of beers or drinks consumed prior to the arrest or accident is a surprisingly low number. The number is two. Now subsequent breathalyzer tests do not support the claims have any basis in reality. We do lie to ourselves and to others about the amount of alcohol we have drunk or going to consume when we go out for the evening. Seldom do we admit that we are going out to get drunk or to engage in the behavior that follows the consumption of alcohol. Getting honest about our drinking is a pre-requisite for sobriety.

JANUARY 2

In Bill's story he writes "There had been no real infidelity, for loyalty to my wife, helped at times by extreme drunkenness, kept me out of those scrapes."* That was true for me and I suspect for a lot of men in A.A. While many claim their sexual desires were increased by alcohol, it is a fact that alcohol is a sedative and sedatives relax people. It is difficult to perform any task when under the influence of alcohol no matter what we might desire. We ought not to pride ourselves on actions not taken if we were in no position to have taken that action in the first place. I've never killed baby seals mainly because I live in a part of the world where they don't exist. I can't take pride in not doing something I'm incapable of doing.

*Alcoholics Anonymous 4th Edition, p3

JANUARY 3

The Big Book states that "Not all of us join religious bodies, but most of us favor such memberships."* It is a good comment that undergirds this organization's desire not to force one belief. The admonition that people of all faiths or no faiths are welcome in A.A. is a valued principle. Yet, I did go back to my faith based on the belief that if I want a spiritual life it is easier to find people seeking spiritual guidance in a church, synagogue or mosque just as I find it easier to remain sober by hanging out with people who are sober. Same principle. You can tell a lot about people by who their friends are.

*Alcoholics Anonymous, 4th Edition. P28

JANUARY 4

The Eleventh Step Prayer attributed to a saint is one of the most beloved prayers found in the Twelve Steps and Twelve Traditions book. Few can or should quarrel with the fundamental message of living and thinking positively. And yet while saying the prayer I am asking to be a willing giver I need to remember that there is a time and place for receiving. I am always in symbiotic relationships when there are times when I need to give to others and there are times when I need to be on the receiving end. There are times when I need to be comforted, to be understood and to be loved. Nobody can give if no one is there to receive. I must learn to receive graciously as well as to give graciously.

JANUARY 5

Alcoholics often refer to the story in the Big Book that speaks of acceptance. The line quoted is that "nothing happens in God's world by mistake"* Well this Bill disagrees and thankfully this isn't a quote from the original Bill. Lots of things happen because men and women using their God given gift of will power make powerful mistakes. The God of my understanding is saddened by our mistakes: Kids are killed in car accidents, people choose to get drunk. There are lots of things God doesn't control. The God of my understanding isn't all powerful but cares deeply about us and the lives we choose to live. And isn't it great that in A.A. no one has to accept my understanding of God in order to get sober.

*Alcoholics Anonymous, 4th Edition, p 417 (1)

JANUARY 6

It is often said that we shouldn't ask God for specific things and that every prayer should end with, "If it be thy will". If we truly believe that we all have a God of our understanding, then this kind of admonition about how to pray seems out of place. I have said that I ask God for all sorts of things, not in the belief that I know better than God, but because I believe that God can be approached in many ways and that he or she is certainly free to say "no". And besides, the serenity prayer asks God to grant us serenity and that sounds like a request to me. The power of prayer is not what God does or does not do with it, the power of prayer points us to where we want to go and what we want to become. Prayer is for us more than for God.

JANUARY 7

"If you want what we have and are willing to work for it" were words that did not sound right to me when I first came into A.A. Who wanted to be an alcoholic sitting in a church basement on a Friday or Saturday night with people who couldn't manage their own lives? Not me. At first all I could see and hear were people who weren't like me. Many had DWI arrests, some had served in prison, some were homeless and without prospects for work. Others had lost wives and families and homes and jobs. None of those applied to me. Now I was in danger of losing my job and with that my home, my cars, my reputation and I had certainly driven drunk a number of times. What I came to respect was that these were all not yets. They were waiting for me if I continued to drink they way I was.

JANUARY 8

"God has a plan for each of us", is one of those remarks I find annoying made by people of good intentions and faith. I do not think that God planned on my becoming a drunk. He didn't plan on people getting cancer either. Lots of things happen to good people and bad people. An old farmer saying was that it rains on the just and the unjust. We ought to be humble enough to recognize that we can't know why stuff happens and not blame God or praise him for that stuff. To say that becoming a drunk was part of God's plan for me doesn't make sense. We enjoy free will not bound by instinct or predestination. It is up to us to make our lives our own. Today I remember that I am responsible.

JANUARY 9

One of the biggest hurdles to get over in our recovery is the idea that "one drink won't hurt you". To our friends who aren't alcoholic the idea of having one drink is so sensible and sound that it doesn't occur to them that an alcoholic cannot handle one drink. We are often asked," can't you have just one?" Lots of newcomers to sobriety who intend to stay have similar thoughts that lead them back to pounding on the bar or kitchen table asking "how did this happen?" To non –alcoholics one drink seldom hurts any of them. To those of us who suffer from alcoholism, that one drink leads to uncountable others. In our hearts we know that one drink is too many and a thousand are not enough.

JANUARY 10

Sponsorship is fundamental to sobriety. Helping others recover helps recovery. The Twelfth Step says that "we tried to carry this message to alcoholics" and one of the ways of doing Twelfth Step work is to sponsor newcomers to sobriety. We laughingly state that helping another alcoholic helps the sponsor more than the sponsored person. But there is a danger in sponsoring people: we can easily fall into believing that we can run that person's life better than he or she can. We need to beware of the danger of false pride when trying to dictate how another person ought to stay sober. There is a danger too that we can too easily fall into the trap of knowing what is best for another person.

BILL E.

JANUARY 11

Easy does it but do it. In the first blush of becoming sober the promise of a "new freedom and a new happiness" is a compelling vision of what the future holds. Who wouldn't want to grasp onto anything that holds forth such a picture of what can be achieved? Some things take time to understand and moving too quickly can result in frustration because that promise is not fulfilled immediately. Until one fully appreciates how unmanageable his life was and what it means to state that we were insane (Step Two) we can move too quickly to want to find out who we have harmed and to make amends. That's why we need a sponsor who can lead us into what doing the Steps really requires of us. Few of us do not need teachers at some point in our educational process. So too do we need teachers in A.A.

JANUARY 12

I like the saying heard in many meetings that one cannot think oneself into right action one has to act into right thinking. Good intentions are not enough. I once suggested that A.A.'s could have produced an excellent electronic game, Intendo, because we were always intending to do things but rarely did them. I was a great intender on bar stools. I intended to get the research done; I intended to get the papers graded. The list was a long one. The road to hell and to drunkenness is paved with good intentions. We have to act. The chapter in the Big Book is titled Into Action not Into Thinking. Imagination is a wonderful human attribute, but unless it leads to something concrete it remains only a wonderful possibility.

JANUARY 13

I'm sober by God's grace and the Twelve Steps. What is the meaning behind the phrase, "God's Grace? As we integrate the 12 Steps in our daily lives, our sense of community is made greater and for A.A.'s that is God's grace working in our lives. I am no longer alone or living such a constricted life limited to booze and its limited companionship As I live up to the principles embodied in the program of alcoholics I find myself at peace with myself and with others. What used to irritate, confuse, and confound me seldom does now. I have been at meetings where the speaker's words reach to my innermost self. I am in that moment hearing God speak to me. And touched by God's grace I want to give that grace to others and in doing so become something larger than myself.

JANUARY 14

Speaking of paths. You can be on the right path and still get run over if you aren't moving along that path. If we are not consciously working the steps of A.A. we are standing and to stand is to get run over by unforeseen events. Life is about change and unless we are cognizant of what is going on around us, we can falter and fail. It doesn't take too much to knock us off course in the physical world; the same holds true in the area of feelings and emotions. Things are great the way they are, so why change or adapt? Because the world is not static and unchanging. New challenges or even old challenges in new guise can distract us and we slip off that path we were on. We need to keep trudging.

JANUARY 15

Remember the worst, before the first is one of those slogans that dominate our A.A. sharing with each other. That is why when I am tempted to wonder what one of the newer alcohol beverages would taste like I recall those words. I know that whatever the initial taste of the fruit flavored vodkas, or the beer fortified with limes or the wines from the new wineries coming on line in upstate New York, the taste for me will soon taste like puke. How many times did I throw up the beverages I had paid such a high price for? Too many to count. Many an evening ended with my head hanging over a toilet bowl with exhortations to God to make the sickness go away. So I remember the worst and don't take the first.

JANUARY 16

Human nature is to cling to that which is illusory and transitory. Why that is I will leave to those who are experts in the field of psychology. Bill W. in writing about this very human trait wrote, "The persistence of this illusion (that the alcoholic will someday be able to drink like normal men) is astonishing".* Bad things happen to other people. A tornado rips through a town and people in the Midwest where tornados are common often express surprise that it happened to their home or to their town. "We never thought the river would rise so high". Denial has survival attributes but the downside can be disastrous. And for us alcoholics denial and living in a state of illusion has proven disastrous until we shake off the lethargy that has kept us bound to old behaviors and take action.

- Alcoholics Anonymous, p.30

JANUARY 17

To illustrate a point I was making I sang a little song and then apologized to the people around by saying, "Sorry, I'm not much of a singer." One of the friends said something to the effect that I wasn't such a bad singer, in fact pretty good. That surprised me because I thought I couldn't carry a tune and judged myself awful as a singer. I wondered if I had changed or if the friend was just being nice. I got to thinking that perhaps I had become a better singer. Prior to getting sober I had attempted to sing the scales but got stuck on do, re, me, me, me, me, me. It's just a way of saying that honesty is great for reducing pride of self. I need to remember the we, we, we of staying sober.

JANUARY 18

Looking back on the more than 24 years I have been sober I value the concept of one day at a time. I couldn't imagine conceiving of not drinking for 24 years when I began. I remember being impressed with a person's nine months of sobriety. That was impressive back then and remains impressive today. We value long time sobriety because it demonstrates that it can be done, but most of us know that time alone doesn't guarantee continued sobriety. Each day is unique and a testimony to the soundness of living one day at a time. Some object to the giving any recognition of time in sobriety and others refuse to claim sobriety in any public way.. This seems shortsighted to me since that which is recognized is more likely to be repeated.

JANUARY 19

In the beginning and continuing for too long of a period of time after I started getting sober I resisted seeking "through prayer and meditation to improve our contact with God as we understood him".* Each time I tried meditating the day's events or the clock sounding in the hallway or thinking about what to have for supper, interfered with my attempt at what I considered meditation. Sitting in a yoga position didn't have any appeal for me either. I have since learned that meditation comes in many forms and can be done in many ways. Meditating can mean focusing on the immediate whether it is washing dishes or strumming a guitar. At any rate when we refuse to meditate we are fulfilling Bill W's comment, "Many of us exclaimed, what an order. I can't go through with it."

*Alcoholics Anonymous, p 60.

JANUARY 20

The Lord's Prayer is one that is that most of us are familiar with. When we ask that God forgive us our trespasses it is only in magnitude to those that we forgive in others. We should not ask for more than we are willing to extend to others. And when we pray, "give us this day our daily bread" it is a reminder that we live one day at a time. Am I okay today at this moment? Do I have what I need right now? That doesn't mean that I do not plan for tomorrow, I just can't plan the outcome. One day we are here and the next we are gone. That is the way for all life and so we need to make the most of the time we have. And due to my own faith I include the words Mother along with Father and use the plural, names when saying that prayer.

JANUARY 21

Step Ten really asks a lot. I have to accept that not only am I frequently wrong but so is everyone else. Can I easily admit that I am wrong? Well, yes when it is obvious, but what about the times when there is doubt as to the cause of the misunderstanding or the argument with someone else? I can be right about my position but still wrong in my insistence that others agree with my assessment. I can be wrong in how I approached the subject or how I acted in an all-knowing manner. Admitting you are wrong when you may be right is really what this Step demands of us. Even when I am not guilty, I can add to the day's serenity by not demanding that my position be affirmed by everyone around me.

JANUARY 22

False pride and ego can still cause me to be embarrassed. I was talking to a newcomer about how nice it is to have money at the end of the month instead of when I was drinking I had month at the end of the money. I told him that I liked to put a $20 bill on the bar to show how little I cared about the money and he replied that he had done similar acts but that he put a $50 bill on the bar. I quickly noted to him that my $20 amounted to the same in today's dollar. Here I was still trying to show off, not wanting to be outspent by some other drunk! How much money was wasted in a futile attempt for big shotism? I can never full account for the wasted fortune spent in this endeavor.

JANUARY 23

Part of the allure of alcohol at least in the beginning was that it was illegal to drink at the age when we started. There may be a few alcoholics who started drinking after reaching the legal drinking age in their state but most of us started drinking in our early teens. Forbidden fruit, in this case usually cheap wine, has always been appealing to humankind. Genesis contains the story of Eve offering Adam the apple to which he ate without apparently thinking about the consequences. We do believe that he had yet to acquire a sense of right and wrong, but we couldn't offer that excuse: we did know right from wrong and the wrong was oh so strong that we capitulated readily.

JANUARY 24

During my first rehab experience the acting department chair where I worked with real sincerity said to me, "Bill, you really are too smart for the A.A. program." Strangely enough I found myself agreeing with her. I was too smart for A.A. Not so strangely I found myself in another treatment program a little more than a year later. What I learned from that experience was that people outside of A.A. will tell you what you want to hear, while those in A.A. will tell you what you need to hear. I don't blame the department chair, her attitude is widespread that intelligence alone can be the basis for staying sober. What most of us learn with disastrous consequences is that knowing alcohol is not good for you is not enough to stay sober.

JANUARY 25

My parents finished formal schooling with the 8th grade and so when mother began warning about the evils of alcohol I thought her warnings illustrated a lack of understanding. Sure, she had lots of brothers and sisters who were drunk a lot but she came from a Southern Baptist background which explained her opposition to alcohol. I would later add lots of initials after my name attesting to my intelligence. But mother's understandings of the effects of alcohol were much better than mine. Alcohol is no respecter of education, gender, and race, religious or ethnic background. Being smart is no protection against alcohol I learned a little late. I should have listened to my mother. In A.A. meetings I try to remember that I can learn from people whose education and background are different from mine.

JANUARY 26

"If you want what we have" were words that grated on my ears in early sobriety. Sitting in church basements with a bunch of drunks on any given evening or afternoon was not particularly appealing to me. Did I really want to associate with people who were widely seen as losers? Not hardly. I saw myself as solidly middle class and in the beginning I blindly saw only people who had lost jobs, family, self-respect, and health. It took time to deflate my ego and to look honestly at what I had become. I was no better nor no worse than my fellow sufferers. Today I am sincerely pleased with members of A.A. who in most cases have all the things I have or on the verge of recovering what they had lost. Who wouldn't want to be with people who are making it their business to live a life free of the bondage of self?

JANUARY 27

The first time my employer thought it wise for me to get sober, I was given the Big Book of Alcoholics Anonymous in rehab. As an academic, I read the front pages and noted it had first been published in 1939, a year before I was born. What could a book that old tell me about alcoholism? I barely skimmed the pages and did no serious reading. Right now was important not the writings from a long ago era. The writers in academic literature are mindful of what had gone before, but scientists would surely not rely on the findings in a book that old. The material wouldn't be cutting edge discovery. It has been said that bias is contempt before investigation. I had forgotten that any scientist who ignored the past findings would be seriously handicapped. So it was for me. When I came in the second time it was with a lot more humility.

JANUARY 28

The tell-tale signs of alcoholism were there, I just ignored them. I remember a friend, surely as a joke, sent me a list of 10 signs that alcohol might be a problem. One that I remember was if you have to have two or more drinks a day, you might have a problem with drinking. My reaction was of incredulity! Two drinks? One at noon and another with your evening meal and you are an alcoholic? My response was then everybody is an alcoholic if it only takes two drinks to get you so labeled. I know now It isn't the number that is important but the having to have the two drinks: when there is a compulsion to have the drinks. I also remember visiting a state park on a Sunday morning with friends and arriving at the park around 10:30 and they opened up a can of beer. I asked," beer before noon? "What difference does time make?" my friend responded. Sounded logical to me and the first of what would become original values being dropped. Sometimes alcoholism creeps up on a person.

JANUARY 29

The statement that I'm a grateful alcoholic sounds strange to people who are not familiar with recovering alcoholics. Newcomers often express surprise that anyone could call themselves a grateful alcoholic. I was painfully reminded of that truism when a good friend died much too early. I met him at the first meetings I attended and over the years the common bond of relief from alcoholism cemented into friendship. I would later sponsor the man through a rough period of time in his life. So, how does this tie in to being a grateful alcoholic? I would never have met Rick nor would my life be as enriched as it is. It has been said that most of us in A.A. would never have voluntarily met each other. Rick and I were different in many ways but we found a way to real friendship. And for that, I'm grateful.

JANUARY 30

Don't compare but relate. That statement always bothered me and unsurprisingly I let my disagreement with those who said it bother me. I thought that comparisons were when you were looking for similarities between two items or in our situation two people. Finally I looked up the terms and the dictionary definition says that comparisons are when you are searching for similarities and differences. I had been wrong about the meaning of those words. The bottom line for me was to quit debating what the words meant and to accept the principle, whether comparing, contrasting, or relating, to focus on how similar I am to other alcoholics not how different I am from them. I discovered that I was one of them.

JANUARY 31

What makes a group a good one? Is it the number of people who attend the meeting? Is it the number of people who are home group members with long term sobriety? Is it the way that newcomers and visitors are welcomed? Is it the ease with which members volunteer for group service positions? Does the group have members serving as Intergroup Representative and in other larger A.A. service positions? Is it the outreach the group does for those in jail or prison or bringing the meeting to a rehab center? Is it the number of times the group visits a homebound home group member? Do group members support each other in times of grief and illness? Is it the amount of money the group sends to a central office or to Box 449? Is it the number of Big Books that the group gives away each year? For an individual the answer is simply, "Does it help keep me sober?"

FEBRUARY 1

One need only pick up any newspaper and be reminded of how powerful this disease is. A young woman driving while drunk, has an automobile wreck and kills a fellow passenger. The normal reaction to causing such a tragedy ought to be to never drink and drive again. The better reaction would be to vow to never drink again. Yet time after time that person will not only drink again, but will drive again. And far too often another tragedy will occur. When we read that alcohol is "cunning, baffling and powerful" we are hearing a powerful truth. Honesty is the bedrock of getting sober and accepting how powerful it has been in our lives is a beginning towards sobriety.

FEBRUARY 2

One of the most freeing aspects of living a sober life is that I am responsible for my feelings and behavior. If I am angry that feeling is often a choice, especially after the initial reaction. The same is true for all other feelings. I can choose to be happy, sad, joyful, and remorseful. When I was drinking I was sure that the emotions I had were caused by other people. A good example of that for me happens when a car in front of me has its turn signals on for way too long. That is irritating to me unless I discover the car ahead of me is being driven by a friend. Then it doesn't seem so awful. I can be taught that other people did not cause me to drink in response to those emotions. The freedom we get is the freedom to make choices.

FEBRUARY 3

Humility and humiliation have much in common but what separates the two is that humility is one that we can choose and humiliation is something that happens to us. Most of us have been involved in situations and behaviors that are humiliating: dancing nude on a bar table, wetting our bed, making statements that are rude, crude and uncalled for, making phone calls one day and not remembering that we made that call the next day, getting arrested for drunk driving, forgetting children's birthdays, wedding anniversaries, missing out on a business appointment. All of these things happen to us because of the choices we have made. They are humiliating. Humility is something we choose when we accept that our behavior has been outrageous and have a sincere desire to change. Humility says that we know only a little and that more will be revealed.

FEBRUARY 4

Challenging a long time member on his behavior or attitude is not often done. Who would feel comfortable stating to a person with long term sobriety that he is engaging in stinking thinking or looking for trouble with his behavior? That may explain why someone with 19 years or 26 years goes back out and restarts his path to misery. No one is immune permanently to this disease: it requires constant vigilance. I continue to go to meetings on a regular basis so I can not only hear what happens when one chooses to drink but so that my friends can help me maintain my sobriety. I must remember on a daily basis that I am an alcoholic subject to the old character defects popping back up in unexpected places. And friends in A.A. shouldn't shy away from pointing out when they see those defects emerging once again.

FEBRUARY 5

Alcohol held out the promise of a sophisticated life: knowing the different wines, what made the top shelf liquors worth what they cost and the discussion of the merits of the ingredients in the various drinks. What it led to for me was public urination against brick walls, sticking my head into the toilet to relieve myself of the alcohol and food consumed and the occasional wet bed and clothing. Television advertising always shows young people with nearly perfect bodies in a desirable setting. Never do they show the end of the event pictured. I need to keep the picture of my last drinking episode in mind.

FEBRUARY 6

Choose goodness rather than evil. Ah, if life was so well ordered that the difference between good and evil could be so easily identified. Usually the choices are depicted as a little fellow with a halo on one shoulder and a fellow with a pitchfork and horns on the other shoulder. Was it bad that I became a drunk? Well it may be good, it may be bad. Certainly the pain I caused family, friends, co-workers and students was bad. But if I hadn't become a drunk then I would never have confronted the character defects that were the source of the pain I caused others. How many lives have I helped because I was in A.A. when they came in? I have no way of telling. But with the little fellows on my shoulder speaking to me means that I made the choice to which one I would listen. It wasn't caused by some outside force.

FEBRUARY 7

After a night of drinking way too much, I would approach the breakfast table with some trepidation. Would my wife be upset or would she greet me with the normal "good morning". If she were angry and upset I would apologize not knowing what was the cause of her resentment. Better not to know than to have to face completely how irresponsible I had been the night before. On the other hand, if she welcomed me warmly, I felt a great deal of relief and breathing deeply promised myself I would not consume that much drink again. That pattern of behavior would be exhibited over and over again and finally recognizing that, I took the Second Step and admitted that I was insane.

FEBRUARY 8

A newcomer asked an intriguing question wondering why so few people seem to remain sober after being introduced to A.A. The easy answer is that many of us exclaimed, "What an order! I can't go through with it", there are other reasons. The person asking that question also indicated that he was there to try to impress the judge that he was doing something about his drinking. He wasn't there to get sober but to get the judge off his back. Many alcoholics come in hoping to get their spouse or employer off their backs or to get back the respect of their children. All of that seems like good reasons to the drinker. As sober members we know that those reasons are not ones that are likely to lead to sobriety. That is why the Big Book points out that unless we have hit bottom, we are likely to drink again. The cliché, that "many may need A.A., but fewer people want it", remains true. Only when we are ready to do the steps can we expect to succeed at getting sober.

FEBRUARY 9

Stating, "I'm sorry", is not making amends. I'm confident that it stems not from a sense of guilt or remorse, but is a lame attempt at getting the offended person off my back. My mother would often use the term to describe a person without worth: "That's the sorriest person on the face of the earth". Now I believe that all humans have an inherent sense of worth but that many of us have squandered our inheritance. It takes real work in the real world to restore our sanity and inherent worth. When we describe the work that A.A.'s must do, we accept that many don't want to do what is required; we want the easier softer way of talking the talk rather than walking the walk.

FEBRUARY 10

Like father like son? These words from an anti-tobacco ad in 1969 helped convince me to give up smoking cigarettes. The words accompanied a picture of a young father sitting under a tree with a pack of cigarettes lying on the ground. The young son picks up the cigarettes and looks longingly at them. We all want our children to avoid the mistakes, errors, and poor judgments that we made. When our children pick up our bad habits we wince with regret and that is especially true when it comes to alcohol. Didn't they see what booze did to their dad or mom? Of course they did, but like us, they are convinced that it won't happen to them. I know that I did not think I would become a drunk like my aunts and uncles, after all I was educated and they were not. Alas! Education and personal observation are not enough to steer us or our children in the right path.

FEBRUARY 11

I have not always been comfortable around men and women who had been in prison. That changed when I visited Attica State Prison for several months and discovered how normal the men in that prison appeared. They were not different in appearance and intelligence from those in a typical faculty meeting. A number of them claimed they had no memory of what brought them there. Some of them were not telling the truth, but I couldn't just dismiss that for everyone as self-serving because I know that I acted out in blackouts and could not remember what I had done or whom I had been with. I have come to know scores of men and women who have been in prison and who are just like me. I must remember that I am no better or worse than any former jail mate.

FEBRUARY 12

How do I know what God wants from me? A good question deserving of a good answer. Very few of us actually hear God speaking to us and in fact people who hear directly from God are not recognized as being of sound mind. How then can I say that God speaks to me? The answer I received in early sobriety was to listen to what is being said in A.A. meetings. How simple and uncomplicated is that approach to listening to God. Just as I read with discrimination, I listen in A.A. with discrimination trying to identify those with long term sobriety who speak quietly with dignity and respect for their own humility. Pompous and demanding are not why I expect from my higher power, but a power calling me "softly and tenderly".

FEBRUARY 13

The fog is an interesting phenomenon evoking feelings of fear and closeness. So it is with the fog of alcohol when it hides the dangers that may or may not be lurking in the denseness of the mists. It can also create a sense of mellowness and safety. When the fog of our drunken loaded minds is lifted we confront all the realities surrounding us in all their stark relief. Now that we can see clearly it is somewhat understandable that we want to return to the fog induced mindset where we didn't know or care what was happening. When the fog has lifted we may not like what we see. What we fail to realize is that even in a fog, harm can come to us unseen and can be even more deadly.

FEBRUARY 14

Most of us recall the good times we had drinking and partying with friends and co-workers. If there hadn't been fun while drinking, few of us would have continued drinking. But it is similar to the Pavlovian dog who when Pavlov would ring a bell and provide a treat or meal for the dog he would begin to salivate at the prospect of the treat or meal. In time the dog associated the sound of the bell with food and the sound alone was enough to cause the salivating. That is much like it was with our drinking and fun. We drank and had fun and in time thought it was the drink that caused the fun. In sobriety we have learned that good times can be had without the drink. Happiness is not connected to drinking.

FEBRUARY 15

A number of religious groups find the insistence that each person is free to understand God in a way that makes sense to them upsetting. A personal belief in God based on personal experience threatens their belief that only a hierarchy can fully explain God to the masses. To some extent they are right. Individuals on their own can rely too much on their own thinking and it was that thinking that got them in trouble in the first place. It is why we have sponsors and why we have home groups. Relying on our own and thinking we can get sober on our own led invariably to failure. All great religious leaders have their own "sponsor" someone they can trust to keep them from going off a deep end.

FEBRUARY 16

Epic stories illustrate the danger and difficulty of relying on sheer logic and will power. Odysseus on his way home from Ithaca would pass by an island of Sirens, women whose voices lured men to their island where the men were shipwrecked and killed. Odysseus had his men fill their ears with wax and to have them tie him to the mast in order to avoid the rocky shores. He knew that at any time and with certain forces he would by himself be unable to avoid the temptations. The same is true for us alcoholics, we can't rely on our will power or our thinking to avoid the temptation of just one little drink. We need the help of a higher power, and we often the need the help of our friends in A.A. Will power alone is insufficient to keep us sober when the siren sound of a single drink lures us away to despair. We say that we should tie a knot on the end of a rope and hang on knowing that we too are a lot like Odysseus.

FEBRUARY 17

The historian Santanya wrote, "Those who do not remember the past are bound to repeat it". We tell our stories for a variety of reason but we do it primarily for ourselves. How did we get to where we are today is essential in every aspect of our lives. Businesses must constantly review past practices, look honestly at their failures and record those errors in order to avoid repeating them. I must not forget what brought me to A.A. I can look back on some of my escapades and laugh at them. Many memories are embarrassing. Many are filled with remembering the danger I put myself and others in. All are valuable reminders of what can happen again if I forget my past. I live in the present, but the present is shaped by my past.

FEBRUARY 18

My sponsor often told me in the beginning to "act as if" which drove me bananas. What did he mean by that? For some reason he wouldn't explain the phrase to me. Slowly I began to grasp the meaning of "act as if". The program is one of action and if we are to get better, we need to act our way into better living. There was a book published a few years ago with the title, The Secret". The premise of the book was that there is a law of attraction and that if you act and concentrate on what you want, it will be yours. Now that is probably a simplistic explanation of the book and there are serious doubts as to its validity in all cases. But if we do want a good life free of alcoholic obsession we need to think and act differently so that we are attracted to the good rather than the bad. Good things come to those who act.

FEBRUARY 19

The past will be your future if you go back to drinking. This warning was confusing at first until I witnessed a number of people who came into A.A., heard what was being said, and returned to drinking. When they came back as some are lucky enough to do, they had gone almost immediately into the same situations that had originally brought them to A.A. I am convinced that all the mental and physical anguish I experienced before A.A. will return if I pick up a drink. It is a lesson delivered over and over again and only a few are destined to learn the lesson that the person who hasn't changed will drink again with the same results.

FEBRUARY 20

"He quit going to meetings. That's a sure sign that he was going to relapse". Well, that may be true but before he quit going to meetings he had probably begun to rely less and less on a "conscious contact with his higher power". We will find ourselves at some time or place powerless against another drink unless we have a belief in a higher power that we can call on. In many cases we need to call on our sober friends. In early sobriety, like many alcoholics I struggled with this whole "higher power" stuff. Higher power is God with a title less burdened by past bad experiences in religious schools or places of worship. Today I use the term, God, without reservation with my own understanding of that higher power.

FEBRUARY 21

I go to several meetings where the attendance is well over 50 people and the donation received is well under a dollar a person. I calculated one night that if those 50 people had been in a bar buying at least three drinks for an hour the total bar bill would have been approximately $600. Now none of those groups need that kind of donation and undoubtedly lots of those in attendance may be hurting financially from too frequent visits to bars, but this little calculation does show how our values are still out of whack. We need to ask ourselves, why were we so willing to spend so much in a bar and give so little to spreading the message on how to stay sober?

FEBRUARY 22

Character defects are like weeds in the garden. You can pull them all out one day and sure enough there are new ones popping up the very next day. Dandelions in the yard are especially amazing as I can cut them down and by the next morning their progeny are standing tall and are often in the seed stage. How can this be? I do not pretend to know the life cycle of plants but I am pretty sure that character defects much like weeds are never eliminated; only kept under control. Some of the character defects are similar to very hardy plants whose roots go very deep. Getting them killed is a difficult task. And so it is with some of my character defects especially the self-centered focus of much of my life. It takes especially hard digging and persistence to get rid of the worst of my character defects.

FEBRUARY 23

For far too long many of us saw things in black or white. That kind of thinking is illustrated when I have said, "If I ever go back out, then I won't make it back it because the embarrassment of facing my friends in A.A. would be too great." When I say that I am admitting that false pride is still one of the character defects that I struggle with. Think of that statement: death would be preferable to embarrassment. Because for me with that attitude to drink is surely to die. It also demonstrates a lack of humility because I have seen countless people with years of sobriety go out and come back in to A.A. They chose life. With God's help I won't test my resolve that I would rather die than admit that alcohol is cunning, baffling and powerful even for someone with my years of sobriety. I need to remember pride goeth before a fall.

FEBRUARY 24

Why is there such an emphasis on humility? Change involves that characteristic plus sacrifice. An admission that what one has been doing is not working whether in personal affairs or in any other aspect of life doesn't come easy. What politician cares to admit that his pet theories or policies have not produced the desired outcome? What businessman likes to drop a product line that is not selling if he had been convinced it was going to be highly profitable? What scientist likes ending an experiment? In every case eventual success means doing just that and success in sobriety means admitting that what one thought were good decisions simply weren't. I finally had to admit that my experiments with drinking were not producing the good life, in fact quite the opposite.

FEBRUARY 25

Complaining about reverse discrimination finally brought a mild rebuke to the speaker. The speaker was going off on a tangent unrelated to alcoholism as sometimes happens in A.A. The line separating personal problems from alcohol related problems is pretty blurry. It is an often expressed value that old timers in A.A. have a special responsibility to keep the discussion on alcohol. It is too easy to fall into thinking that every problem we face or every issue that we care about or every topic can be related to our problem with alcohol. That isn't true. As caring individuals we hesitate to interrupt a speaker, but if we really care about A.A. we need those sometimes brave souls to keep bringing us back to the essence of why we are meeting: how can we help the still suffering alcoholic. A.A. meetings must not be allowed to degenerate into gripe sessions about wives, children, politics, religion or any aspects of living life on life's term. I later thanked the person who stopped the complaining about reverse discrimination and promised myself I would be more responsible in taking appropriate action when necessary.

FEBRUARY 26

Don't do for your sponsee what he can do for himself is good advice. Once our minds have had the fog lifted we can see more clearly than before and the natural tendency is to help others see as clearly as we now see. As recovering alcoholics we want to help our fellow sufferer avoid the mistakes we made. It is very similar to raising children. They must find their own way with our direction but not our command. Our program is one of suggestions even for those we sponsor. Very few people in our culture respond happily to being told what to do even with the best of intentions. Healthy sponsor and sponsee relationships are grounded in mutual respect and love. Demands seldom work among the most enlightened of us and humility demands that I accept that I cannot always know what is best for someone else.

FEBRUARY 27

Debating was one of the joys of my academic and personal life. In high school, college and as a high school teacher who taught debate I reveled in the pitting of one idea against another. It is a good way to discover the truth and to settle arguments. Debating is a good mental challenge keeping the debater on his figurative toes. When it came to alcohol I didn't debate. I did not look at the facts or the consequences of my behavior or the behavior of others who drank too much. Somehow my keen mind wasn't up to the task of collecting data that would challenge my actions. Too late I learned that I should have been debating the affirmative side of the debate: Resolved that Bill cannot safely drink.

BILL E.

FEBRUARY 28

Doubt is a major stumbling block to sobriety: Am I really an alcoholic? Can one drink do me in? Is A.A. the best way to get sober? Can I really learn how to be sober by a bunch of drunks? Is sobriety all that it is cracked up to be? All good questions and merely asking them indicate the high probability that the answer is yes to every one of those questions. I wasn't really asking them in a serious manner but in what would prove to be a vain hope that I could wiggle out of the answer I didn't want to hear. There are other ways being promoted to getting sober including the ever present hope that some vaccine or medication will remove the compulsion to drink. I ask myself today, "Would you go back to drinking if you knew you could do it safely?" My answer is no. What is the reason for drinking if you couldn't get drunk? You see I am an alcoholic of the worst kind.

FEBRUARY 29

Do you have to go to those meetings the rest of your life? Who knows for sure? I do know that there are people who quit drinking with the help of A.A., seldom if ever go to meetings and remain sober. Whether their life is as good as it could be is another question. I continue to go to meetings due to the explanation I heard early in my journey to sobriety: I want others to have the same chance that I had and for that I am responsible. Spirituality to me is helping another human being and no where is my help more greatly needed than in helping others overcome this disease.

MARCH 1

Strange isn't it that many of us choose to be in a church basement on a Friday or Saturday night? The image is not one of sophistication or great fun. I so wanted what alcohol first promised me: sophisticated drinking and knowledge of what makes for Top Shelf liquors, great wine and fine food. What it eventually led to was public urination, inability to recall what I had drunk and the puking of some of most expensive food on the planet. Sticking my head in the toilet bowl does not conjure up the image any one has of sophistication. Sophistication was not all that it was cracked up to be. I prefer the less sophisticated surroundings of a church basement. Life can't get any better than it is today, but I wouldn't have believed that 24 years ago.

MARCH 2

Beauty parlors promise to erase wrinkles, hide skin imperfections, reduce the signs of aging and help us present to the world a vision of ourselves we want to portray. A lot of us try to live as if our physical imperfections can be hidden under cover and to some extent that is true. We can get away with signs of aging with effort and expense. Eventually we have to accept that we are wrinkled, gray, and have brown spots. Would that our spiritual imperfections and character defects could be so easily erased, heaven knows we tried to cover them. Eventually we had to accept that the defects of character needed more than cosmetic work. Cosmetics only work on the outside.

MARCH 3

Adult beverages. If ever there was a misnomer that is one. What alcohol did to me was to reduce to me to a child-like stage where certain body functions requiring diapers would have helped avoid discomfort and embarrassment. The first drink I ever had was offered by a farmer friend of my dad as I helped work with a bunch of men on a hot July day. "Bill", he said, "you can have a beer with the men, just don't tell your mother." Two things appealed to me with this offer; one that I would fit in with men and the second and probably more appealing was getting away with something mother didn't want me to do. Hiding one's behavior is not the action of an adult but of a child. So, for me, it was never an adult beverage.

MARCH 4

The game of chicken is one of the dumbest games one can participate in. Think of it. Challenging another person to do something potentially life threatening on a dare, just to prove what? That the winner is somehow stronger or braver than the one who quits at the last possible moment? My alcoholism had elements of that. I continued drinking when someone said, "oh come on have another one." Or the individual who said, "one drink won't hurt you", or "hey, I can drink you under the table." All of those are a lot like the game of chicken. "Quitting early, chicken?" All of those old taunts kept me behaving recklessly endangering my life and those who would later cross my path in the automobile I would drive home after a night of heavy drinking. At the time I couldn't see how foolish the behavior was and only in retrospect do I shake my head at how I reacted to such heckling. Chicken is better than dead.

MARCH 5

"They" is a pronoun covering a lot of blame. "They" caused me to be angry. "They" caused me to make a mistake. "They" caused me to get behind in my work. "They" caused me to do a dumb thing. When I dropped the third person pronoun and adopted the personal pronoun, I for my anger, my mistakes, my failure to get work done on time, then I became able to get over the anger, stop making so many mistakes and got my work done on time. A.A. emphasizes personal responsibility and that makes the program difficult for many to accept. For all the vaunted cultural emphasis on individuality most of us hide behind the ubiquitous "They" until each of us accepts that we have no one to blame but ourselves.

MARCH 6

Staying vigilant is tough. Discomfort occurs, attention to detail slips, forward movement requires effort and the desire for respite is tremendously challenging when the laziness causes us to rest on our laurels. Why do people struggling with sobriety have so many slips? Few of us get sober on the first try. Mindless and thoughtless repetition of the familiar has become engrained in us. Practice does not make perfect it makes permanent. Permanent is more difficult to change than the transitory. Until we practice the principles of the program so that they are as normal as breathing, we will continue to find staying sober a tough assignment. Hundreds of thousands of recovered alcoholics show that it can be done.

BILL E.

MARCH 7

We are like the Little Red Hen of children storybook fame. She could find no one to help in growing the wheat for the bread but was quickly surrounded by those who were willing to eat the bread after the work had been accomplished. How often did we sit in bars lamenting the advances our friends and co-workers were making? How often did we say that they were kissing up to the boss rather than facing the fact that we were unwilling to do what they were doing? I like the statement, "if you want what we have" since it applies to all aspects of our lives not just in recovery. Am I willing to do what my co-worker who got the promotion did and am I willing to admit that it was work rather than favoritism? Am I willing to do what is asked of me in A.A? Tough questions requiring honest answers. If I want the bread then I must do the planting work.

MARCH 8

"I'm trying to get sober", is an interesting position. My initial reaction to such sentiments is that you either are sober or you are not. Upon reflection though I'm a little less critical and have come to recognize that trying new behavior, changing thought patterns, leaving behind old haunts and friends is part of that trying to get sober. Sobriety is more than just not drinking. We all know people who are what we lovingly refer to as on a dry drunk. We have to change our behavior and that requires effort, failing to do what needs to be done and learning from that failure, becoming willing to ask for help, listening to the suggestions from fellow alcoholics and reaching out to other alcoholics with whatever strength and hope we have achieved so far. Those are ways that we are trying to get sober and are absolutely necessary if we are to arrive at that place called sobriety.

MARCH 9

Somehow I knew that my behavior was less than sterling; that I was bringing grief and unhappiness to those I love. I thought I could make up for the transgressions by being really good at cleaning house or repairing broken objects or going to church or changing diapers or doing the hundreds of little things that have to be done in any relationship. I wanted credit for doing mundane things to balance against the debits piling up. The inequality in this balance lies in the reality that I was determining what the credits were worth, mostly exaggerated, and the debits, mostly undervalued. It did not come to me that the person I was indebted to placed a different value on those credits and debits.

MARCH 10

Newcomers are often confused at the laughter they hear in A.A. meetings. After all this is serious business, this getting sober. What could possibly be funny about the behavior that has led us into A.A.? The laughter stems from our realization that, while not funny at the time and not funny for those around us, it is funny that we thought the behavior normal. We must be careful though not to let laughter become a means by which we judge the value of the speakers' stories. We are not there to be amused, that is not the point of telling what happened and what it was like. When we laugh it is a by-product of our story not the main intent. If nothing tragic happened as a result of our behavior, no one died or was permanently disabled, then we can rightly laugh knowing that the line between humor and tragedy is indeed a narrow one.

MARCH 11

"Assets can be noted with liabilities" is a good suggestion from the Twelve and Twelve. Very few people if any are willing to change their behavior if they only hear what is wrong with them. An inventory in any business is finding out what is no longer selling or useful and finding out what needs to be added and kept. The same is true for our Fourth Step inventory. Find out what has brought pleasure and happiness to you and to others. Where have you felt most useful? Are you good at helping others? When did others praise what you had done? Just remember in taking the inventory that while much still needs to be eliminated, you are not completely awful.

MARCH 12

If your God was self reliance no wonder you eventually failed. No one is an island unto himself and cannot possibly hope to be self sufficient or rely only on individual skills. There is an interdependent web of life that means that every living thing is connected to each other. The idea is summed up in the song, "Circle of Life". In addition I depend on the electric company to provide power, for the trash collectors to pick up household refuse, for teachers to teach my children, for the police to provide protection for the doctor annual checkups. The list is endless. So, why is it any different when it comes to personal issues of health and well-being? When I depend on my friends to keep me humble then I can truly do what I am uniquely able to do.

MARCH 13

Everybody dreams of being calm and at peace with himself. The struggles of everyday living can be enervating but we also need the quiet of the night. Without sleep or rest, we simply could not live. Our challenge then is to have this balance in our lives. With alcohol running our lives we simply could not be at peace for any length of time. We may have confused passing out with peace, but it was a tortured peace at best. Quieting the mind so that the peace of God can enter is necessary and why we call for moments of silence in A.A. meetings. It is difficult but not impossible to hear God in raucous surroundings, but it is easier if we quiet our mind amidst the hurly-burly of the day.

MARCH 14

William James, an influential psychologist for early A.A.'s wrote" The greatest discovery of my generation is that human beings can alter their lives by altering their attitude of mind. ..If you change your mind, you can change your life". This powerful insight propelled Bill Wilson and Bob Smith in creating Alcoholics Anonymous. That is also why they also wrote that A.A .has no monopoly on truth and that we must remain open to clear perceptions and findings of others. More will be revealed was their gift to keeping A.A. relevant and helpful. We should not limit ourselves to reading only conference approved literature for revelation is not limited to just a few.

MARCH 15

The central neurosis of our time, emptiness, was observed by Carl Jung another pioneer in psychology that A.A. owes much gratitude. If emptiness was a central neurosis 70 plus years ago it is no less so today. Recovering A.A.'s speak of a hole in their innermost self that they attempted to fill with alcohol and drugs. The more we tried to fill that hole with chemical substances the bigger the hole seemed to get until we admitted complete defeat and a willingness to try spiritual means of filling that hole. When we worked the Twelve Steps and when we focused on helping fellow alcoholics did that hole begin to shrink. Emptiness is no longer making and keeping us sick.

MARCH 16

"How can I know what God's will is for me?" is the plaintive cry from beginners and sometimes even stated by those who have been coming to A.A. for years. In Step Three when we are asked to make a decision we ask what that means. In Step Six and Seven we are ready to have God remove all these defects of character and then humbly ask him to remove them. As most of us know, it seldom happens that they are removed. Does that mean that this is a waste of time? Religious leaders of every faith struggle with knowing God's will and with a few exceptions we certainly are not religious leaders. Accepting that God's ways are not our ways means we continue to struggle with understanding. After several thousand years of the stories in the Bible and hundreds of years of the Koran we continue to read and work to make meaning of the writings. We do the same with the Big Book.

MARCH 17

Great literature is forever applicable. The Bible lasts because beyond all the challenges to it when it was written and the historical accuracy of the stories, the text is always old and new. We read Shakespeare, the U.S. Constitution, and Ernest Hemingway because they speak to us as much today as when written. The Big Book of A.A. is great literature precisely because it fits the definition offered for great literature. Readers continue to find new meanings in paragraphs highlighted in previous readings. What was at first reading ignored is underlined after the second reading. The references to events in World War II or to iron lungs does not distract from the essential message that the Big Book is forever new.

MARCH 18

This is an honest program. No one can get sober based on living lies. Yet we also have to try doing and saying things that sound strange and not quite true when we get sober. Take the question of "did you feel like drinking today?" Well you may have but instead of saying yes, try telling yourself a new story, "No, I didn't feel like drinking today". And feeling like drinking is different than wanting a drink. In both cases we need to say something antithetical to the true answer. Is that lying? No, we are acting and thinking as if we are sober. Actions can change our thinking and our behavior.

MARCH 19

We may be surprised a lot after we are sober for a while. Where are we in the family pictures and family movies? Wasn't I there? Well you may not remember whether or not you were at family picnics, holidays with family and friends or at other family outings. You may have been passed out or not there at all. The absences are a good reminder of what you have lost and why you want to change. And then of course there are those pictures and movies where we were there all blurry eyed and looking ridiculous. Those pictures are a good reminder of what you were like, what happened and a reminder of the bottom that brought you to A.A.

MARCH 20

Admitting that we are powerless over alcohol is easy. Many of us stated and acted with false bravado while drinking. "I'm a drunk; alcoholics have to go to meetings". That admission is not enough to get sober because we have to accept that second part of the first step—that our lives had become unmanageable. And furthermore even that is not enough for sobriety. "Yeah, my life is screwed up, that's the way it is and will be. Whose life is a bed of roses anyway?" Sentiments like these will keep us from doing the First and consequent Steps.

MARCH 21

"Why did I do that?" How many times did I regret my actions and my verbal responses to people, places and things? Actually none of us know the answer to the embarrassing situations and awkward statements. We may have apologized profusely promising ourselves that we would not do that again. All too often the apology and situation faded into the background and we found ourselves once again wondering why we behaved and talked that way. I don't think I truly understood how far I had fallen from the values and principles I purported to support and follow. In sobriety, for instance, I found that my neighbors didn't really think my ethnic humor was all that funny nor were the ribald stories in mixed company all that amusing.

MARCH 22

Recovery takes time. If that is true for us and it most certainly is, then recovery for those family member, co-workers, neighbors and friends will also take time. When they are skeptical of our sobriety they have every right to be skeptical. We have not been exemplars of honesty prior to quitting drinking and made too many unfulfilled promises to change, to not drink so much, to act graciously that this time seems no different than before. We may feel hurt because wives or husbands want to smell our breath or to wonder why it took so long to take the trash out. That is old behavior. Acceptance is the key here along with a further strengthening of our contact with a higher power that in time they too will believe.

MARCH 23

Don't make a big deal out of making amends. Not at first at least. Start with small acts demonstrating you are different. Do things without asking, volunteer to help where you haven't helped before. Clean up your language. Offer to give foot and back rubs. If offering and doing these acts make the other person uncomfortable understand why and back off. And don't expect expressions of gratitude. There will be ample time to work the Fourth Step and to look at the major shortcomings. Just remember that beginning on day one, you can start to practice different ways of behaving. That is the reason the 10th Step says that we continue to take personal inventory.

MARCH 24

A friend of mine died recently from cancer. He discovered this only by accident and after the cancer had a head start on destroying vital organs. There were no warning signs or at least none that were easily recognizable. Our disease shares some similarities with cancer. It can creep up on us without easily recognizable attributes. Who doesn't enjoy a night out celebrating with too much to drink? Or there is an occasional blackout but we all experience some forgetfulness even when not drinking. Each of these alone is not enough to cause great concern—lots of people experience them without dire consequences. Then, like my friend's cancer, the disease is in full bloom. Unlike cancer, alcoholism can be reduced to a state of remission with full recovery dependent on doing a few simple things.

MARCH 25

Our emotional sickness can be treated with some pharmaceutical offering. We may temporarily reduce its influence with pills but eventually we need more than what the drug can do for us. Psychological research indicates that talking through our problems is probably more effective than any of the modern medical offerings. They have further noted that without the talking the pills themselves are not effective. So, what Bill and Bob discovered decades ago without modern research continues to be supported by research that's as modern as today. They either knew intuitively or through the guidance of a higher power that one person sharing their emotional failures and listening to each other can be the most powerful medicine one can take for this affective disorder.

MARCH 26

Courage overcomes fear. We are no longer afraid of real and imaginary threats to our existence. We are facing the challenges that everyone faces: financial insecurity (the rich for example fear losing what they have and the poor fear not able to meet everyday needs). Facing those we have harmed rather than fearing what they will do to us requires courage. We can't predict the outcome of these encounters and rely on the experience of those who have made this courageous act before to guide us. Relying on our own resources has not proved successful in the past and we cling too long in the delusion that this time we can do it without help. Together we can accomplish more than acting alone is a lesson we need to remember.

MARCH 27

A Chinese proverb: When someone shares something of value with you, and you benefit from it, you have a moral obligation to share it with others. Remarkable isn't it that what Bill and Bob established with the program of Alcoholics Anonymous is shared by other countries from other centuries. The principles of A.A. are grounded in the intelligence that came before us. Those of us who have been blessed with the gift of sobriety as a result of the work of the founders and countless others who followed and shared their "something of value" have a moral obligation to be there when others need the understanding that we have received.

MARCH 28

Henry Adams, a noted educator wrote that a teacher's influence affects eternity as no one can tell where the influence ends. In a sense those of us who have been in A.A. for some time and live the program of A.A. are teachers for those coming in to A.A. after us. And it is not the subject matter that is important as much as it how the teacher interacts with the students. We teach not by the words alone but how we treat our sponsees and fellow sufferers. When we practice the principles in all our affairs we are teaching by example. Let us never forget that our actions speak louder than words.

MARCH 29

Expect to win is the attitude every coach and player must have in they are to succeed. The same is true for us recovering from alcoholism. We use such phrases as "keep coming back" and "you have nothing to lose but your misery" as a way of saying expect to win. If you keep saying I can't do this then the chances are pretty strong that you will not be able to do this. We read from the Big Book "many of us exclaimed what an order. I can't go through with it" when in fact it not that we can't but that we don't want to. A positive attitude in dealing with physical health problems significantly increases the chance that the individual will recover from the physical ailment. Why would we think that treating alcoholism would be any different? We shouldn't.

MARCH 30

Disappointment is a fact of life. No one succeeds all the time. The best baseball players hit the ball one third of the time. Few of us are good at every subject in school. Financial advisers are wrong more often than they are right. Will you stumble on your road to recovery? It's not a prerequisite but it happens. The best runners will pull a hamstring, stagger and bruise a knee. The person we want back in our lives refuses to come back despite our amends and change in behavior. Our character defects will rear their ugly heads and cause us setbacks. Experience is a good teacher since we learn as much from failure as we do from success. As an old song goes, "pick yourself up, dust yourself off, and start all over again."

MARCH 31

The ancient Greek philosopher, Epicurus wrote the good life is one that is marked by moral, prudent and honorable behavior. The Twelve Steps of A.A. are aimed at our learning how to be moral, prudent and honorable. The golden rule, forgiving others, balance in all endeavors are new ways of acting for those in early recovery. We have not thought of those we love and who love us, we have behaved badly taking advantage of others, and we have often spent money unwisely. How do we then know what is moral and prudent and honorable? We depend on the help of others in recovery and that in itself contains those three recommendations for living the good life.

APRIL 1

Both our reasoning and our intuition will tip us in the wrong direction from time to time. Every person occasionally needs someone in their life that will call them out. What we did to ourselves would have caused outrage if someone else had treated us the way we treated ourselves. The harm we did to others is matched by the harm we have done ourselves. We have pushed through life as if we were the only one that counted and we have left behind ruins that will take time to rebuild and restore. The person who decides that he's going to get physically fit makes a mistake if he expects it to happen with one burst of energy. So it is with our recovery.

APRIL 2

We can be surrounded by people who love us, people we work with, neighbors and friends and still be isolated. That doesn't seem possible at first reading. Upon deliberation it really isn't so odd. Have we really let anyone know our deepest fears and frustrations? Have we kept these to ourselves in order to present a picture that is not true to who we are? If people really knew what I do will they really like me? Often we allow only a minority of people to know these fears and failures. If a friend, co-worker, or family member ever said, "what causes him to be like that", you can be assured that isolation is at the heart of the mystery.

APRIL 3

Why is confession to an alcoholic so useful? The usual answer is that only the alcoholic can really identify with another alcoholic. I think there is something deeper than that operating during this acknowledgment of the harm we have done others. There is the implied reality that the confessor and confessee share similar if not identical stories and carries less chance for condemnation. This is especially true when the confessor admits that he has done the same thing. There is something healing that connects one human to another when we know that we are not unique.

APRIL 4

Technology changes are challenging to the spiritual foundation of A.A.-our anonymity. There is a lot less stigma attached to alcoholism or drug addiction than there was when A.A. was founded yet it is not completely gone. I doubt that there are few families that have not been touched either directly or indirectly by drug and alcohol abuse. Anonymity is still the foundation and as long as an individual does not openly proclaim his alcoholism or that of someone else, then the foundation is still there. We are anonymous not just for the sake of A.A. in general but because our egos can lead us to bigshotism.

APRIL 5

What was your role in the situation are words sure to evoke a strong response. Not just from those of us in recovery but including almost everyone else. The response is almost always negative. It seems natural that we see ourselves as victims rather than perpetrators or co-responsible for conditions not to our liking. This response begins early in life with childish blaming our older or younger sibling for the breaking of a treasured item in the home. She was chasing me or she pushed me or she got me angry. We lost a job because someone was jealous of us. In A.A. we accept responsibility for our reaction and our behavior no matter how egregious the behavior of the other person. Believe me; it's not easy to say I was wrong. Non-alcoholics may get away with being the victim—we ought not to try.

APRIL 6

How we perceive or interpret events creates our reality. When we infer that any behavior either ours or someone else's without checking how others see the activity, then we are on shaky grounds. It is now widely accepted that eyewitnesses to accidents are notoriously wrong in what they saw. Two people looking at the same accident can see completely opposite factual details. If this is so, and especially in highly charged events by bystanders, then who are we to completely trust our own observations and interpretations? We may be correct but we need to temper our responses and assertions with a degree of humility accepting that we may in fact be wrong. "I may be wrong" is a good place to start.

APRIL 7

Accusations that you are drinking sting when you haven't been imbibing. Instead of reacting with anger it may be a good time to look at our behavior. Stopping drinking as we well know is only the beginning of sobriety. We have to have a complete personality change and that doesn't occur without a great deal of effort and backsliding. Our old behavior has been ingrained so that the behavior is automatic. A good response is to ask the accuser what makes them believe that. We do not argue with the accuser. We may very well not be aware that the old manners are asserting themselves. Our unconscious mind may be doing us in.

APRIL 8

Laughing at ourselves is healing. Laughing at others is not healing. Laughing with others is healing. And what we laugh at is important. We do not laugh necessarily at the events that marked our lives as active alcoholics but at the reasoning we relied on to justify the behavior at the time. That is one of the grounds for challenging our reasoning—it didn't serve us too well in the past. In the end we must rely on a higher power often speaking through our friends in A.A. to guide us in sobriety. And so we laugh at how we ever could have done the things we did while thinking we were sane.

APRIL 9

Are we worthy of sobriety? Strange question to ask ourselves but the fact of the matter is that the question is asked of us in perhaps a less stark manner. Our old drinking buddies may try to convince us that our lives suck and have no meaning and that getting sober won't change anything. They are likely to dredge up all your old justifications for drinking. And then the cruelest and dumbest statement may be, "you think you're better than us!" For this reason alone we need to immerse ourselves in A.A., getting a home group and a sponsor to provide needed moral support when we are most vulnerable to old ways of thinking.

APRIL 10

Masquerade parties can be fun as long as there is a beginning and ending to the parties. What happened is that we took on masks to keep people from knowing who we were with all our imperfections. The party never ended for us as we wore the masks out of fear that we weren't good enough, smart enough, and good-looking enough for the people we associated with at work, home or play. In time we may have cut ourselves off from other people fearing some unnamed and amorphous danger to our psyche. What we were doing was damaging ourselves by refusing to accept ourselves as creatures of a loving God with inherent worth as any other individual.

APRIL 11

A.A. doesn't ask you to do anything before they teach you how. They teach through a very powerful educational process—by example. Sit in any A.A. meeting and you will hear how other people have worked each and every one of the Twelve Steps. How do you turn your life and will over to the care of a higher power? First you get to choose an understanding you have of a higher power and if you don't have one, adopt one of someone else. Secondly you don't have to come to that understanding all at once. How does one contact that higher power? Always the recommendation is for simple prayers. Help and thank you are simple and direct openings to prayer. In every one of the preceding and following Steps the process is similar.

APRIL 12

Misery loves company. A lot of us after starting the path to sobriety will occasionally go back to our old haunts believing mistakenly that we can be with old acquaintances and not drink. One of two things will happen. We will try to join in the conversations with a cola and soon decide that one drink won't hurt and we're back and running. Or, we find ourselves uncomfortable and leave. The former drinking partners are not impressed with our new found sobriety and probably resent it and want us back doing what they are doing. Or, when we leave we have made the decision to no longer be in the company of misery.

APRIL 13

"Don't get mad, get even", was an epitaph from a well-known politician. It sounds so good and right, doesn't it? Getting mad never solved anything and is not a healthy response either. But neither is the second part because it extends the pain of the first bad encounter to another one. The responses could be endless much like the fabled Hatfield and McCoy battles. The better response is to forgive and forget and that is one of the many recommendations that we in A.A. respond to when someone says, " I can't do that." If we are to change this is one of the ways can do so. It is seldom easy getting and staying sober.

APRIL 14

Only wet babies like change was the title of a sermon in a church I attend. A.A.'s are not the only ones who resist change but we probably hang on to old behaviors long after any benefit has ended. Think of the times we drank for fun and relaxation. Good benefits for anyone. We also know that the fun and relaxation came to an end. We were drinking not for fun and relaxation but because we had a mental and physical compulsion to continue the dysfunctional behavior. Like babies we must embrace change for comfort and for health. And like babies we need help in doing so.

APRIL 15

"Hey, I was drunk!" That was an excuse that would work a few times in the beginning of this disease. It soon wore off as we piled up event after event. That we even thought it would continue to work is amazing in retrospect. If, after making a fool of ourselves and used the I was drunk excuse, we quit getting drunk the excuse would have been acceptable. But time after time? No, like every other excuse we offered, this one's welcome wore thin. When we accept responsibility for our actions through the Twelve Steps of A.A, we quit excusing our behavior. We accept the responsibility to make amends.

BILL E.

APRIL 16

Who is this other that we might have harmed? In making direct amends to those we have harmed we should consider ourselves as one of the other. While we may have lied about hurting only ourselves we did hurt ourselves and we may be carrying some of that hurt into sobriety. I was physically, mentally and spiritually bankrupt when I came into A.A. In order to get better I had to take action in each of those areas of bankruptcy. A.A. helps with the mental and spiritual part of my hurting and that leaves me to do work on the physical impoverishment. Like everything else in sobriety, I took it easy and began daily walking beginning with half a mile a day gradually increasing distance. A sound mind in a sound body makes good sense.

APRIL 17

Albert Einstein noted that, "We can't solve problems by using the same kind of thinking we used when we created them". What better slogan for recovering alcoholics could there be? When we are told that we must change everything first among those changes must be our thinking. We kept thinking that there must be a "softer, easier way" of ridding ourselves of the problems brought on by our drinking. We kept thinking that this time it would be different that there was some source of our problems outside of self. Slowly and surely we came to the conclusion that the problem was within. And our thinking was most definitely within.

APRIL 18

Character defects are a funny thing. Well, maybe not funny but at least present a paradox. For instance it is considered good character to be generous but we can be generous to a fault giving away to others so that our immediate family suffers. We can spend time helping another alcoholic and ignore the needs for our closeness and help for wives or husbands. We can be angry and stop a terrible injustice from occurring and anger can bring destruction to personal relationships. We need to be generous but not to a fault, we need to spend time with alcoholics but give time to those closest to us and we need to be angry but direct it to good ends. In all things we need to practice the golden mean.

APRIL 19

Willingness is not enough. Sure, we have to be willing to change but that key to recovery must be matched with an understanding of the price that must be paid. We cannot refuse to use that key because it is going to cause us pain. Am I willing to change even when I know that pain will result? We often choose the pain of the known rather than the pain of the unknown. When we choose present pain we are really expressing fear—fear of the unknown. We have to step resolutely forward trusting in the experience of those who have gone before that this too shall pass and that the pain of changing is worthwhile.

BILL E.

APRIL 20

We're a noisy culture. Think of the elevators that play music, that when we are put on hold with the telephone we receive sales messages or music, the televisions running in our homes with no one watching. It is no surprise then that we have trouble meditating. Getting quiet so that we can listen to the still small voice is difficult. How many times have we heard in A.A. meetings," I can't stand the silence" when a topic has been announced and there is a period of quiet before anyone speaks? "All the exhortations to be still and listen seem to fall on plugged ears. We need the silence to hear our higher power.

APRIL 21

Words soak into our ears when whispered not yelled. One of the saving graces of A.A. is the principle that this is a program of suggestion rather than coercion. No one can demand that you do anything in A.A. and this is the source of much discussion among those not familiar with the emphasis on our leaders as trusted servants. All of us are servants to fellow A.A.'s. Tough love is recommended but the emphasis ought to be on love not tough. We know only a little about the person just coming into A.A. One approach for all people doesn't make sense based on what we know about human motivation. We can be gentle and speak softly to the hurting alcoholic recognizing the old bromide that you can catch more flies with honey than you can with vinegar.

APRIL 22

It doesn't take a strong person to hold a grudge. In fact the weakest among us can carry them quite well. We need to let go of old resentments and anger and grudges. The grudges keep us from fully recovering. As long as we let someone else's behavior dictate what we are thinking and feeling, that is as long as we keep from making a positive change in our lives. We remain dependent upon someone else and remain mired in the muck and mud of all that has contributed to our sense of frustration. We know we cannot change someone else and when we let these grudges dominate our thinking, we are giving control over to that other person.

APRIL 23

My biggest troublemaker watched me every morning from my bathroom mirror. Truer words cannot be made. Oh how I wanted to blame the people where I worked, my wife, my neighbors and strangers on the roads I traveled. Metaphorically speaking I hated the sunshine because it exposed the shadows in my life—those secrets I would barely if at all admit to me let alone others. I lashed out at those who would bravely say to me that my behavior was not acceptable. Only when I came into A.A. thoroughly beaten by alcohol would I begin to listen to those whose experience, strength and hope could help me. Even today I must be aware that words of wisdom can come from many sources and my willingness to listen is paramount.

APRIL 24

Referees make a few bad calls in every game. As far as I know there has never been a perfectly called ballgame. One side or the other will claim that at least one call wasn't a good one. Occasionally even a referee will admit that he missed a call. The game goes on even with cries of "We wuz robbed". The fans and players have to move on or the whole game or season will be lost because of a bad call. Can you imagine a team walking off the court or field after that missed dub and refusing to play until the official end of the game? Well, we can't refuse to play the game of life because we've had a few bad calls. We have to get over it. That is why we must forgive those who have "trespassed" against us. We need to get on with the game.

APRIL 25

I notice a bad smell coming somewhere in my living room. I look and look and discover that my dog has apparently had an accident. Do I just ignore the odor and dog dropping or do I find some way to pick it up and dispose of it? I think the answer is pretty obvious. It is the same principle with our character defects. Now that we have learned what they are we should be willing to get rid of them which is what the Sixth Step of Alcoholics Anonymous is all about. Dog droppings are not going to be removed by a higher power; we will have to do the disposing. With character defects we can call on our higher power to help remove the defects because they are much more entrenched than dog droppings in the house.

APRIL 26

Leave me alone, I'll be all right. Oh, how we fooled ourselves. There are many things we can do for ourselves after a night of drinking too much. We can get a cool compress for the head, take an aspirin and lie quietly until the pain eventually goes away. It will take more than a cold compress or aspirin for the thing that brought us the need for them. The fellowship of A.A. is essential for most of us in recovery. Few can quit drinking entirely on their own. If we are honest, we have tried a number of times to quit, to reduce the amount we drank or to promise ourselves that we won't do that again. The failure rate for this approach is nearly 100 percent. Why does relying on others to help us present such a problem when this is clearly a softer, easier way?

APRIL 27

Pruning is a necessity if shrubs are to flourish in our yards and gardens. Some branches become too gangly while other branches die and sometimes the growth is too much for the plant to sustain. Cutting away is the way to maintain proper balance and to ensure good life for the whole plant. We too must prune away that which is threatening our good health and appearance. The act of pruning does require forethought and careful consideration just as our pruning away the excesses in our life must be done with care. The temptation in early sobriety is stop smoking, overeating, start exercising and doing other healthy actions, all in an attempt to quickly make a difference. Here is where the A.A .slogans Easy Does It and First Things First come into play. Nothing else matters if we don't get sober and trying to do too much too soon almost guarantees failure.

BILL E.

APRIL 27

Once we have accepted that we are an alcoholic we begin to revert to some old ways of thinking. Some of us try to differentiate ourselves from other alcoholics by adding the adjective, real, as in" I'm a real alcoholic." Now I'm not going to get too exorcised over this self definition since it is better than saying that I'm just a little bit alcoholic. And surely some of our bottoms have been more brutal and deeper than others, but I think it is a lot like being a little bit pregnant; you either are or you aren't. Let's be careful that when calling ourselves a real alcoholic that we are not feeding our egos. Even the description, I'm a garden variety drunk may be veering close to setting oneself apart from others and making us special in our humility.

APRIL 28

It is inevitable that old resentments will pop back into our minds every so often. We spent an awful lot of time and energy with them before joining A.A. and those get imprinted in our memory. What do we make of this phenomenon? Well, don't fret– this will pass- and get on with recovery. The best response is to laugh at how this once consumed our life and that it now only gets a passing reference from the memory bank. Pray to your higher power thanking him for relieving you of the daily obsession you once had with those resentments.

APRIL 29

It felt good breaking the rules. Underage drinking meant taking a risk with mother and dad and perhaps school authorities. The thrill of getting away with something prohibited by adults was a powerful motivator to drink alcohol. It also meant bonding with the people we were with at the time and in the case of males it was a sign of masculinity. I could be one of the good old boys. We value independence in our culture and this was one way of showing that we were independent of adults. What we failed to recognize at the time was that we were becoming dependent on our peers and eventually dependent upon a substance that would drastically alter our lives.

APRIL 30

Gratitude is an action word. That may not sound sensible at first as gratitude is viewed as a feeling of thankfulness for favors received. For those of us in recovery gratitude calls on us to do more than just have this feeling of good will towards those who have saved us. Just as "I'm sorry" is often not enough in making amends, "thank you" is not often enough gratitude. In amends we do something to repair the hurt we have caused and in gratitude we do something to return the favors we have received. Actions speak louder than words and we are called to take action to demonstrate how thankful we really are. Begin with the words thank you and follow up with asking how to return the favor. In A.A. our gratitude is best expressed in helping another alcoholic recover.

MAY 1

"Made direct amends wherever possible", is an expectation of our program of recovery. Lots of time making direct amends is impossible due to deaths, geographical distances and the sheer number of people we have hurt without knowing. If, as a teacher, you were less than prepared for class or took no time to know your students, you cannot make that up to them directly. Indirect amends is a way to atone for the past infractions in those cases. Give blood to the Red Cross, volunteer at a school, help at homeless shelters. The list of community groups needing help is large and is a way of giving indirectly for the pain caused the nameless others.

MAY 2

A simple thank you to the newcomer or the person you are sponsoring can be more powerful than the usual response," you're helping me more than I am helping you." We ought to be grateful to the newcomer because we know that helping another alcoholic is the best way to stay sober. We also have a responsibility to show the newcomer how to live and thanking people for the help they are providing makes for a powerful lesson on how to live a sober life. Simply saying thank you is showing the newcomer how to behave. Practicing the principles of A.A. in all our affairs means that we have a duty to demonstrate how good and decent people live a life worth emulating.

MAY 3

"My sobriety is worth more than all the money in the world", is a little bit over the top. First of all we are not going to be offered all the money in the world and so we will never be faced with that choice. I know that the substance of the statement is that without sobriety we have little chance of enjoying whatever good things come our way. That statement to the newcomer probably causes him to question your sanity since to him the good things money could bring to him or her sounds awfully appealing. Not knowing what awaits him in sobriety, "beyond your wildest dreams", the newcomer will choose the known over the unknown. Better to state the obvious, life without sobriety is not a life at all.

MAY 4

The GPS (Global Positioning System) is a wonderful technological device. Using it means that no one will be lost anymore. No more excuses that we made the wrong turn or went down the wrong highway. We know where we are at all times. That is if we use it and listen to it. Otherwise like other modern marvels, we will remain stuck in old ways of doing things if we ignore what it is telling us. The parallel to A.A. is striking isn't it? Sure, A.A. is not a modern marvel of brilliance, but doesn't it mean that we won't be lost anymore, make the wrong decisions and not know where we are at all times? The danger is that we will revert to old ways of getting around in the world ignoring the direction we are receiving.

MAY 5

"How do you eat a cow? One hamburger at a time!" This is just another way of saying "one day at a time". Most of the seemingly huge tasks can be handled if we take them one day at a time, one step at a time. When I joined a local fitness club they provided a computer generated program that recorded my progress. The first time I read the summary that I had lifted one elephant on my first two visits, I laughed. Then I saw the wisdom of the approach of one elephant at a few hundred pounds at a time because it kept me motivated. We need signposts of our progress and many A.A. groups provide coins or chips representing the first twenty four hours, then a month and on and on as we succeed at staying sober a little bit at a time. We use whatever it takes to stay sober.

MAY 6

The mirror on the wall and the photo in the album can be cruel. Through these means we can see ourselves as other see us. When we were drinking the reflection and the picture spoke volumes about how physically sick we were. The mirror was broken or the lighting distorted our image or they caught me at a particularly bad moment were the excuses we offered for what was painfully clear. If we believed what we were seeing we might have changed our behavior. Like so many other messages these two were often ignored or downplayed. Only when we get honest with ourselves are we able to make the changes we need to make.

MAY 7

Don't let the God written about in A.A. literature keep you from forming your own understanding. Take the phrase", there is one that has all power that one is God." The God of my understanding does not have all power or if he does then he chooses not to use it. The God of my understanding mourns with us over the loss of a loved one; he desperately wants us to take the action necessary for living without being controlled by Bacchus. . I don't think God wants kids killed in cars driven by drunken parents. A caring father does not want to control his children instead preferring to show by example and message what ought to be done. That's one facet of the God of my understanding and you're free to use it or refuse it.

MAY 8

"He's checking his list and checking it twice, going to find out who's been naughty or nice". Ah, the old Christmas song about Santa Claus. There couldn't be a better admonition for us doing the Fourth Step. We have powerful "forgetters" and we are also deniers often claiming we have only hurt ourselves until we have done the Fourth Step. It is probably a good idea that we check out this list with our sponsor and spend time doing it so that we have given enough thought about our past behavior. Checking it twice should be reminders that like all the other Steps we come back to it as we continue to work the Steps in our daily lives.

MAY 9

The saying that membership in A.A. ranges from Park Avenue to the Park Bench is a different way of stating the obvious, that alcohol is no respecter of money along with a disease that hits all gender, ages, ethnicities and intelligence. The rich may have an even more difficult time of recognizing their alcoholism as they may have better ways of avoiding the reality that alcohol is ruining their lives. Money may keep you from sponging off your friends or stealing from your parents or running up bar bills that become troublingly large. In A.A. meetings though, the rich show up as often as any of the rest of us.

MAY 10

Reports from health departments indicate that deaths from drug overdose are rapidly growing and may soon reach the levels of deaths by car accidents. Part of the reason for that is that death by car accidents are on a steady decline due to among other reasons, seat belts and air bags. Death by alcoholism remains a number one killer in the United States. Seat belts and air bags save lives only if they are used. A.A.s metaphorical seat belt and air bag, the Twelve Steps, can only save us if we use them.

MAY 11

Tourism plays a major economic role in many parts of the country. We Americans love to travel in search for new experiences and new understandings. Tourism is good for mental growth too. And A.A. also has our share of tourists, people who come in for a short visit, don't like what they see or hear and move back to the safe comfort of the known. Many who visit us may not belong in A.A. and by any fair assessment are not alcoholics—people who do not suffer from the compulsion and craving familiar to alcoholics. Yet for many more of those who visit, they either find the A.A. meeting not only a great place to visit but one that encourages them to move here permanently. Open meetings provide a place where men and women can visit and decide for themselves.

MAY 12

Magical thinking got most of us into A.A. and won't get us out of our alcoholism. There is something childlike in having a lucky rabbit's foot, special stone to rub, or in believing that there is an elf out there with a pot of gold at the end of the rainbow. And there is nothing wrong in hoping that lady luck will shower us with her beneficence. Sometimes wishing seemed to work—the cop didn't pull us over, the spouse didn't know when we came in last night. But hoping and wishing didn't really work. It takes effort to rectify the mistakes of the past and to make amends. We need to give up the childlike desire for effortless success.

BILL E.

MAY 13

It's matter of when, not if, you will think about drinking. The natural state of an alcoholic is to be either thinking about drinking, drinking, or getting over drinking. What happens after when the thought of a drink crosses the mind is what matters. You can accept it as part of what it means to suffer from this disease and then get busy and distract yourself from the thought. Or you can somehow try to justify why the thought of a drink appeals to you at that moment. When you are trying to justify that thought you are allowing the thought to control you. Remember you are free of the mental compulsion to drink as long as you are spiritually fit.

MAY 14

Everything in A.A. requires work including getting spiritually fit. Most of us would be laughed out of town if we tried to get physically fit by thinking alone. Think yourself thin sounds appealing too but I've never heard that it actually works. Two simple things require losing weight—less food and more exercise. Thinking yourself spiritual sounds appealing too but I've never heard that it actually works. Getting spiritually fit requires two simple things: stretching—reaching out to help another individual and knee bends—praying to your higher power. And remember that prayer takes many forms—even on our knees. Bending down to help a youngster in a reading program is an example of prayer in action.

MAY 15

A friend of mine claims that he was often kidnapped by aliens, beings that took him away for hours and sometimes days at a time. How else could one explain those periods of time that he couldn't remember where he had been, who he might have been with and what he had done? A good number of us had the same experience but we noted that they came after way too many drinks and had nothing to do with aliens. These blackouts were an early warning sign that "wet brain syndrome" was a likely outcome of continuing our excessive drinking. Yet, like adolescents we thought we were immune from such an outcome. Those of us now sober, realize how we dodged a bullet.

MAY 16

Autumn for those of us in the northern hemisphere is a great time of the year. The foliage of trees and bushes brighten each day especially when the air is crisp and the sky is blue. Autumn for those of us in the northern hemisphere is a sad time of the year. The turning the leaves from bright green to fading colors remind us that death comes to all of us. Which view is true and which one do you embrace? We are in charge of how we view the world and how we interpret it. In July we will complain when a day's temperature reaches 60 as being cold and in December will remark on how warm 60 is. We don't need to be Pollyannas always seeing the bright side of events but we don't need to be the opposites either.

MAY 17

I'll get by with a little help from my friends could be the anthem song of A.A. A.A. is often called a self-help group whose members hold that without the fellowship they couldn't stay sober. Most of us tried numerous times to quit drinking only to fail repeatedly until we found that one alcoholic helping another alcoholic helps keep both of us sober. The common precursor to relapsing is missing meetings where we find the help and encouragement we need. Very few individuals in and out of the rooms of A.A. can quit on their own. Honestly looking at one's attempt to quit, slow down or manage in other ways our drinking illustrates quite vividly that A.A. members need a little help from their friends.

MAY 18

Have you ever tried to get rid of fruit flies in your home? They are extremely difficult to eradicate requiring persistence in sprays, washing of counters, removing fruit to the refrigerator, slapping them with swatters and opening windows to chase them out. Still, they remain. Just when you think the fruit flies have been defeated, some new ones start flitting around. I compare them to our shortcomings which show a similar resistance to removal. You cannot just learn to live with them because they will grow and reproduce just like fruit flies. So, eternal vigilance is required both with fruit flies and shortcomings.

MAY 19

If you are having mechanical problems with your automobile, you can work on the car yourself and if the problem is a minor one or one you have the requisite skills, you can fix the problem. If you are having living problems, you can work on self by yourself and if the…you can finish the sentence. A mechanic, someone who has worked on cars similar to yours, is probably your best bet. So it is with A.A. Men and women who have worked with people like yourself is probably your best source for fixing the problem. If the mechanic tells you that you need new brake pads you ought to get new brake pads and not decide that you need new lug nuts. If your sponsor tells you that you need to get down on your knees and thank your higher power, you ought get down on your knees and not decide that you can be all right with reading a meditation pamphlet.

MAY 20

Jesus once replied to a question." how often should you forgive someone? The answer, 70 times 7, seems excessive. I mean wouldn't you begin to look rather silly since the behavior kept being repeated? Few of us forgive and then forget except in minor matters. We will remember, no matter how hard we try, slights and harm done to us. Each time we remember the behavior that caused us pain, we need to forgive again and again. That is the way to humility and acceptance. Once is not enough in most cases as we surely recognize the continuing influence of our past. We are human and have all the frailties' of our species. We are human and have the strength to continue to forgive not only for the other person but for our own sanity.

MAY 21

Faith can move mountains but bring a shovel is an oft-repeated saying. We can also accept that mountains can be moved pebble by pebble implying that small persistent efforts can also eventually make big changes. Most of us do not like the slow but steady labor asked of us preferring big changes that are immediately noticeable. These big noticeable changes feed our ego and make for dramatic changes. Sadly, the big changes are seldom followed up by the necessary work to maintain the dramatic alteration. Old behaviors creep back in because the necessary foundation has not been prepared. Then comes disillusionment and failure. Try the pebble approach to change.

MAY 22

Put your pants on one leg at a time. There really is not a simpler way of doing this. Does anyone ever really try putting pants on two legs at a time except for comedic purposes or to try to prove that it can be done? This is another way of saying keep the A.A. program simple. What is asked of you does not require any complicated way of getting sober. Follow the suggestions made by people who may have tried other ways of getting sober and have found the simple steps of A.A. to work every time they are seriously tried. Many will try to find a softer easier way of putting on pants or getting sober. Believe the old-timers. A.A. is the simpler way.

MAY 23

As far as we know today drug abuse and eating disorders are not the same as alcoholism. Eating disorders primarily stem from poor body image and results in too little or too much food. Drug abuse seems to stem from personal problems that lead to drug abuse. Alcoholism never stems from drinking too little and our personal problems stem from alcohol abuse. In some cases they may be linked, no question about that. Many individuals suffer from multiple problems of living and certainly some alcoholics overeat and some are recovering from drug abuse. After recovering from alcoholism we can continue to eat without any more concern than the normal person. It seems that most drug abusers can continue to drink after recovering from their addiction. Not so for us alcoholics.

MAY 24

As fate would have it was an old excuse for explaining my behavior. When I had been in A.A. for a period of time I recognized that fate had been another word for God just as luck had been. When the author of the Big Book says that inside each individual is a concept of God I think this might be what he had in mind. Always the source was outside of my ability to control or change events. The unmanageability that characterized my life were these outside controlling forces. Slowly and surely I came to recognize that fate and luck were of my own making and that there was a force that could manage my life better than the false gods of fate and luck.

BILL E.

MAY 25

In joining A.A. we continue to make choices. I was given the choice of having dismissal proceedings begin or to begin a program of rehabilitation. We can choose to follow the suggestions or not. We can choose to go to meetings or not. We can choose to read the Big Book or not. Like the choice I made to begin a program of rehabilitation, the or not choices did not appeal to me. The choices begin with a big IF as in if I want to keep my job, if I want to get sober, If I want to get the judge off my back if I want a life worth living. All too often many who try A.A. won't make the positive choice and choose death, institutions or continuing to wallow in desperation.

MAY 26

Wile E. Coyote could be the poster picture of active alcoholics. He continues to chase the Roadrunner despite overwhelming evidence that he will never capture the elusive prey. Alcoholics continue to chase the elusive feelings we experienced with the first drink. Despite overwhelming evidence that that feeling will never be captured, we keep trying different ways of trying. We get hurt just as Wile does but keep bouncing back to try once again. The cartoon character and alcoholics though differ in one respect—Wile always bounces back and sadly much too often, alcoholics do not unless they quit the chase. I resolve not to be Wile E. Coyote.

MAY 27

If you are biting your tongue you are not being patient. Patience without judging the situation is a powerful tool for sobriety that needs to be nurtured. Like so many other areas of changing our behavior this too doesn't come easily. Practice calming our minds so that the committee in our heads is not dictating our behavior and thinking will take effort. You can practice a recommended meditation practice of breathing in and breathing our consciously. In time, with the help of your higher power you will have control over that committee. What we have called unmanageability in the First Step is becoming manageable. Our tongues are less sore the longer we are sober.

MAY 28

It all depends on the emphasis you give to certain words and the inflection. Upon being greeted at an A.A. meeting someone asked playfully what are you doing here? I replied that there was nothing better to do that evening. On one level that sounds as if I were there from a sense of boredom. Upon reflection though there really is nothing better to do than attend an A.A. meeting! At a meeting I meet with people who are working to solve a common problem, who genuinely like each other, who provide great insight to problems I may be experiencing and whose stories sometimes entertain but always illuminate. So, yes, there really is nothing better to do.

MAY 29

We are strange people in many ways. We want endless excitement and desire perfect peace. What greater contradictions can there be? The lure of the nightclub and the corner bar promised fun, boisterous talk, lots of laughter and the excitement that at any time some altercation might break out. We thought that life would be dull without that scenario. Yet, we also wanted nothing to disturb our pattern of living believing that if only others would act rightly we would be doing great. Quit bothering me was an all too common refrain. In time we will have a good balance of excitement and peace in our lives.

MAY 30

We were adrift on a turbulent body of water in a boat without a rudder. Without a higher power we were condemned to float without direction never knowing where we wanted to go and no means of getting there if we did. Aimless wandering can be worthwhile giving one a chance to discover new places and new experiences. We do not need always be goal driven. At some point this is not enough and we have missed opportunities to be of service to others and to ourselves. As humans we must be purpose driven at some point in our lives. Booze keeps us from the rudder we all need.

MAY 31

Our ability to laugh at ourselves is apparent in what we say we would have been good at doing. There are those who say we would have made great undertakers since we were so good at burying our feelings and covering them up. There is always an element of truth in these observations if not literally true. Unlike the subjects of real undertakers our feelings did not stay buried and kept reappearing at the most inopportune time usually when we drank and our defenses were weak. Today we know that covering them up or ignoring them only leads to further misery.

JUNE 1

"I don't deserve this" is said in two different situation—one where we got something we didn't like or got something we thought we weren't worthy of getting. In both cases we seem to know what is good or bad for us and when we made these claims we were subtly admitting that a power greater than us existed. Something beyond our ability to control things was operating. If we look closely at those situations that cause us to make those statements, we have taken some action that led to those conclusions. This is the essence of taking a moral inventory—discovering our assets and liabilities and accepting them without further judgment.

JUNE 2

Difficulties are part of life. We seem to forget that facing them offers a chance for wisdom. Wisdom comes from struggling with what to do and reflecting on that struggle. Few if any inventions spring forth without some degree of trying different approaches and lots of failures before the final product is made. Why then would we hope to have a life free of any obstacles to our progress? The few people who have everything given to them often lead a life of dissipation. When we pray for wisdom we are asking our higher power for those very experiences that lead to understanding.

JUNE 3

Our lives are not like the weather where there is nothing we can do about it. We can do something about our lives; they are not written in advance and preordained as to their outcome. The choices we make are our own and reflect our values. When we drink we are turning over our choices and values to King Alcohol. Our vaunted independence is lost and we become serf- like. If we cannot say no and mean it and if we cannot do anything without alcohol involved then we are much like the medieval man who could only do what the master demanded.

JUNE 4

Staying on the path is a good idea as we are likely to get distracted by side issues and lose our way. There is another danger though in staying on the path that goes unrecognized; if we do not keep moving then we are likely to be run over by unrecognized events. This is another way of saying that yesterday's sobriety will not keep you sober and that continuing to work the steps keeps us sober. We need to accept that each day requires that we do the steps necessary for becoming the person we want to be.

JUNE 5

Seconds and inches is how the speaker at an A.A. meeting described how he had avoided some real disastrous events while drinking. A few seconds later he could have killed someone or a few inches more and he would have been upside down in a river bed. I recall waking up to the sound of tires hitting gravel just as I hit a mailbox. I came to rest on the opposite side of the road avoiding hitting another car and possibly killing someone. Our jails are filled with individuals who didn't avoid tragedy by seconds or inches. Many of us shudder at what could have been and are grateful that seconds and inches saved us from a lifetime of sorrow.

JUNE 6

Hit your knees didn't make sense to me the first time I heard the expression. Even those of us whose understanding of God doesn't require such bending of the knees it nonetheless is a good exercise. For one thing it does ask for a degree of humility before a power greater than ourselves which overall is a good thing for anyone to experience. I resisted until I thought of the number of times I had been on my knees in the bathroom sticking my head into the toilet bowl and begging for relief from the sickness and the head pounding I was experiencing. I had been brought to my knees by a power greater than me—King Alcohol.

JUNE 7

"How much have you lost to your addiction to alcohol?", was a question directed to us in the rehabilitation clinic. Years later I realized the question was really the wrong way to get us to own up to the true cost of our addiction. Did we really lose the trust of the employer, the friends we had, the house, car, boat, the love of our family or did we give them away? Much too often we gave them away so that we could continue to drink as we wanted to drink. "I got along without them before I met them and I can get along without them now", was a refrain borrowed from a country song that expressed our defiance. Only when we hit bottom did we realize what we had given away.

JUNE 8

What is a sufficient reason for quitting drinking? In story after story recovering alcoholics relate stories of parents who were killed by a drunk driver, a drunken family member who molested them, the violence in the home and the embarrassment family members caused them. Many of us vowed that we were not going to be like that—we weren't going to drink. When we say that alcohol is cunning, baffling and powerful we have no better case than our picking up the drink in spite of what we had seen and experienced growing up and the vows we had made to ourselves.

JUNE 9

Expectations are premeditated resentments. When others won't do what we want them to do we are setting ourselves up to feel bitter about their refusal. The wives who won't do the dishes when we want them done, the husbands who refuse to dress for the occasion, the teenagers who refuse to clean up their bedroom on our schedule are all examples of how our expectations can lead to resentments. We may be so used to making demands instead of requests and cooperatively figuring out how to live and work together that we have either lost or never learned teamwork. Authoritarianism is awfully attractive for its apparent simplicity. Experience shows that this seldom works in the long run.

BILL E.

JUNE 10

No one can seriously argue against balance in one's life. We ought not to spend all our time at work or play. When I hear that someone in A.A. starts mentioning that she needs balance in her life she is often hinting at the idea of reducing the amount of time going to meetings or doing other A.A. work. And I am not arguing for anyone to go to meetings around the clock even if available in your immediate geographic area. What I am suggesting is that the person making the statement of balance ought to check the motive behind that statement and to check with her sponsor as to how much balance she needs as it relates to A.A. Few of us die from overwork and even fewer of us die because we are too involved in A.A.

JUNE 11

Childhood stories that I really liked were when a person found a bottle on the beach, rubbed it and a genie appeared promising to grant the person three wishes. In most of those stories getting the three wishes didn't always work out for the best, there was some price to be paid. I think it is part of human nature to hope that we can get something for nothing without any effort on our part. We sometimes used our higher power before coming into A.A. in the same way—an entity that would magically end the problems we had created. We learned that this higher power could do wonderful things if we did the leg work. Our problems didn't disappear suddenly as a result of prayers. Oh, it is true that it seemed that God answered those prayers when the police car for example wasn't after us after all. We need to be reminded that good things like bad things may not be a result of our wishes.

JUNE 12

A lesson I learned on the farm has stood me well in A.A. As a young boy I would gather eggs and sometimes the eggs were marked so that we would leave them in the nest to hatch as chickens. I thought I would help a young chick pecking its way out of the shell by peeling away some of the shell for the chick. I didn't realize that the chick could only develop the strength needed to survive by doing the work itself. The chick died as a result of my "help". Like the chicken we need to work through the problems and issues in order to become strong enough to live soberly. As sponsors we cannot do the work for the newcomer.

JUNE 13

Rationalization is a major stumbling block to sobriety. We can rationalize the most blatant hypocrisy. As a joke illustrating this hypocrisy is the explanation one man gave for his cheating on his wife: It would be wrong for him to limit himself to just one woman when what he had to offer could be shared with so many other women—making many people happy rather than just one. Seen in bold print we can easily recognize this as rationalization. That is why writing down our character defects and shortcomings may be essential for our full recovery.

JUNE 14

It is often said that we have had a change of heart when we start on the road to recovery. And to a large extent that is true in the non-literal meaning of the phrase. The heart is a symbol of our spiritual life. We also have to have a change of the mind—a symbol of our ability to reason. We read the Big Book and recovery literature, listen to fellow sufferers in meetings and talk with our sponsor in order to achieve a change of the mind. In helping another alcoholic we are doing spiritual work. I am convinced that we also need a change physically—not just ending the putting of alcohol in our bodies. We need to exercise to further heal the body.

JUNE 15

"You were a tough nut to crack" was written on my 9th anniversary card from my home group. How I resented that statement! My first reaction was that that wasn't true. I was failing to recognize how much I was like every other alcoholic who came into A.A. Even after 9 years I still thought of myself as somehow unique and different from others although I would never publicly admit to such a shortcoming. That is why we have the Tenth Step—the daily taking of our inventory and a humility to accept others assessment of our sobriety. What that statement showed me that even after 9 years in some ways I was still "a tough nut to crack".

JUNE 16

"Who am I and what am I doing here", is a good philosophical question recovering alcoholics need to ask themselves. Who am I asks that we confront our shortcomings and our behaviors which indicate how self-centered, egotistical and fearful we are. That is a good question when doing the Tenth Step. The second part of that question asks what we are doing to continue to grow? What are we doing to improve our lives and the lives of those around us? The answers do not always come from self assessment—we need the help of those who we trust to give us honest answers. The questions can also provide us with laughter when we realize that in a drunken state we might well have asked the same questions but with a whole different reason for asking them.

JUNE 17

One of the largest home improvement stores has a selling point that you don't have to do it alone; that their employees are there to help you every step of the way in home improvements. Too often though customers want to rely on their own knowledge and skills and sally forth convinced they can make the repairs without help. If any of us watch some of the real estate programs on TV we know that the number of botched jobs is rather large. Why this insistence on going it alone? Who knows for sure? But like the number of botched repair jobs, the attempts to repair one's life without outside help lead to botched attempts to get sober.

JUNE 18

The best advice you can hear is to get off your bottom and start doing the work you need to do to recover. If you take that advice you will accomplish at least two good things: the exercise you need and the emotional growth you need. Beyond those two obvious reasons is that you will not have to reach another bottom. Whatever brought us initially into recovery, the fact is it was a bottom for us. We have to be knocked on our bottom figuratively if we are to accept the program of A.A. If we harbor any thoughts that the next time, won't be as bad as the last, we are only kidding ourselves. Experience has shown that it only gets worse, never better.

JUNE 19

Sleeping under a bridge, urine-stained pants, and two days' growth of beard, a long coat and a paper sack with a bottle of cheap wine in it is the picture many males imagine an alcoholic is. Therefore, since none of those apply to him, well, obviously he's not an alky. Thus do we lie to ourselves and avoid facing the truth that alcoholics come in many shapes, sizes, ages, shaven or unshaven and who drink wine in the finest crystal and live in fine suburban homes and aren't only men. That reality shakes us as we come to our first A.A. meetings and meet people calling themselves alcoholic. Surely these people can't be telling the truth about themselves we tell ourselves. This is when we first begin to acknowledge that we might belong here.

JUNE 20

Things are simpler when you don't have to worry about the truth. It's an interesting question whether or not we were lying to ourselves about how alcohol was affecting us or whether we were kidding ourselves. I preferred the term kidding since it seemed less loaded in its application to me. Kidding implies a less serious transgression than lying which is why I liked it. The truth of the matter is that the lack of honesty was keeping us from being genuine. It was simpler to avoid the unpleasantness that accompanies the truth. When we admit our shortcoming we face up to the unpleasantness that marked our drinking.

JUNE 21

Is A.A. all there is? We should never refuse to get help from any reputable source: Some of us suffer from mental health issues that are outside the competence of members of A.A.: some of us have financial issues with the I.R.S; there are marital problems outside our domain. Even with alcohol we can accede to professional counselors. We should be mindful that our ego, even about Alcoholics Anonymous, can lead us astray. There is no one way of doing things. Each of us can truthfully say that A.A. is all I need with an emphasis on I rather than you.

JUNE 22

Who's going to stay sober? There is no way this can be determined with anything approaching certainty. The most seemingly hopeless cases of individuals, who have struggled for years, coming into and out of the rooms with discouraging regularity, can and do find their way to long term sobriety. Men and women who have lost little in material terms repeatedly lapse and are matched by men and women who get sobriety with the first serious attempt. The lesson in all this for me is to quit trying to decide who will make it or not. I have no crystal ball to help me predict the future.

JUNE 23

We're all better than the worst we've done. As much as the necessity for the thorough inventory identifying those character defects is, we need also to recognize that our alcoholism is not the totality of who we are. The Big Book doesn't illustrate how to list our virtues but the Twelve and Twelve gives us greater assurance that this is part of our inventory taking. We do recognize that our ego may encourage us to dwell more on the positive aspects of our being, but a thorough inventory isn't complete without accepting that our bad behavior is not the sum of who we are. Humility in the face of this compelling reality would do us well.

JUNE 24

"You're too smart for the A.A. program", were words that I welcomed with enthusiasm. The chairperson of my department meant me no harm, but her words led me back to drinking. Oh, I don't blame her because it is what I wanted to hear. That is a major difference between well meaning friends and co-workers': the former will tell us what we want to hear and the friends in A.A. will tell us what we need to hear. Very few of us want to admit that when it comes to alcohol, we lost our ability to discern the difference between the two verbs, want and need. Today I know that no one, including me, is too smart for A.A.

JUNE 25

We try to practice these principles in all our affairs. That principle is a good one and for me is exemplified by morning workouts. When I start running either outdoors or on the treadmill I never say that I am going to run 5 miles today but invariably I do run that distance. I use the principle of one step at a time. I set out to run one mile or ten minutes and add the next miles and minutes as I continue to run. Setting what seems as impossible goals, staying sober the rest of our life, is usually setting us up for failure. I can handle one day at a time and I can handle one mile or ten minutes at a time. This is practicing the principle of one day at a time in my daily affair of running.

JUNE 26

Mistakes are good! The Washingtonian Society was a precursor to A.A. formed in the 1800s. They believed that alcoholics could help other alcoholics stay sober. They eventually destroyed themselves by getting involved in outside issues—slavery, women rights and the temperance movement were the three big ones that led to acrimony and the ending of this first approach to sobriety. The founders of A.A. learned from that mistake and created the Tenth Tradition where A.A. has no opinion on anything other than alcoholism. And like every good lesson, we hear it repeated at every meeting. As individuals we also learn from mistakes, our own or others. We need reminders too, a good reason to attend meetings.

JUNE 27

Making amends means more than expressing remorse. The word means that repairs must be made—mended. When we recognize that doing the Steps requires this kind of action, we initially assert that we can't do it. There is nothing inherently wrong with saying that we are sorry for our actions. Our problems stem from the fact that we said those words hundreds of times in the past and went right on doing those sorry things. Our believability quotient is pretty low when we come into A.A. That is why we don't immediately start trying to repair the damage of the past other than the very important one of not doing those things we label as sorry.

JUNE 28

"You just don't understand"! We sincerely believe when we start on the road to recovery that the reason we drank was that we were uniquely challenged by events outside of us. We were the victims of a conspiracy to make problems for us. "They" were against us. Slowly and sometimes quickly we came to realize that our problems were of our own making and then and only then were we able to accept help from a higher power and the members of A.A. Now that we are sober we recognize the absurdity of that claim. "Where did I screw up today?" is a good question to ask ourselves as part of the Tenth Step.

JUNE 28

A fear of rejection is at the core of our character defects. Many of us began drinking because our friends egged us to. It didn't take much "egging" for me to participate. Quite honestly I wanted to fit in and belong. Who wants to be an outsider? Who can resist at an early age of development? Very few people can resist for very long. Forget all the excuses slick advertising showing people enjoying life with a drink enticed me to drink. Advertising didn't cause me to drink. The fear that others would make fun of me for being a chicken was the main reason I chose to pick up that first drink.

JUNE 29

The warnings of a loving mother were dismissed. She knew the heartache caused by gin and other alcoholic drinks. But what do old folks know about life in the present moment? I wasn't going to turn out like her brothers and sisters who drank themselves silly. No! No! I was stronger and more intelligent than to become like them. It is that insidious thought that I was different than others, stronger, more intelligent, and more careful than her siblings that lay at the core of my alcoholism. And you know it wouldn't matter if I was stronger, more intelligent and more careful. A.A. is full of people strong, smart and careful, but when it comes to alcohol those characteristics matter little.

JUNE 30

We believe our fears and those fears become the stories we tell ourselves. A children's story concerns a chicken who becomes convinced the sky is falling because a walnut falls on its head one day. She quickly starts telling all the other animals that the sky is falling and soon the whole barnyard is convinced the sky is falling. Only when one brave animal starts questioning where the story started does the fear subside as it is discovered that only a walnut has fallen. We are like the chicken; believing things on scanty if non-existent experiences. Checking with others is a good way to reduce those stories and fears.

JULY 1

We believe that we are due more than we are getting. This often unfounded belief is the source of much dissatisfaction and an excuse for drinking. When we tell ourselves that we are not getting paid enough, that we are not appreciated enough at home, that we are being cheated out of our due inheritance we are setting ourselves up for self-pity and resentment two destructive character defects. When we take our inventory on a regular basis we will discover our part in not getting what we think we ought to have. As in all other aspects of our inventory this can help us correct our stinking thinking.

JULY 2

The alarm clock is a wonderful invention. It arouses us from our sleep so that we may begin the day. There is a mechanism built into the clocks called a pause button that when activated gives you 10 more minutes of sleep and can be used several times in a morning. Putting off the inevitable doesn't change the fact that we have to get up. I guess we could just stay in bed and never go to work. Putting off the inevitable reckoning of our drinking doesn't change the fact that we need to get sober but I guess we could just stay drunk. Sadly some people do make that choice.

JULY 3

No is a word that we may have heard a lot when we were drinking. "No, I don't think you can borrow my car". "No. I don't think you can watch the children this afternoon". "No, I don't think I can go out with you". We were denied simple acts of kindness and we were not capable of performing the simplest acts of kindness for our family and friends for good reasons. When we get sober and stay that way the word no is replaced with yes. When we speak of the gifts of sobriety, we can count the word yes as one of those gifts.

JULY 4

The princess in the story of the princess and the pea could not sleep well even on a pile of mattresses because of a simple pea at the bottom of the pile. She was so sensitive that this slight bulge brought her great discomfort. Okay, this is an exaggeration but it makes a good point about our own behavior. When under the influence of alcohol we could not tell the difference between slight and real offences overreacting to the behavior of others. A smile or laugh could be seen as making fun of us for example and would lead to confrontations with the offender. We would assume that every conversation going on around us was about us. We were princesses.

JULY 5

Every so often a scientific study is announced that holds the promise that a cure for our addiction may be possible. There is strong evidence that some part of our brain is apparently the focus of our addiction—much like when the Big Book states that the problem centers in our mind. There is either going to be a treatment affecting that part of the brain or there may be a vaccine or pill that will make it possible for the alcoholic to drink without causing the mental obsession and physical craving. I hold no objection to such efforts hoping that other ways may be found to help the suffering alcoholic. I do know what works for me. And no pill or vaccine can eliminate the character defects that led to my drinking.

JULY 6

"Humpty Dumpty sat on a wall, Humpty Dumpty had a great fall. All the kings' horses and all the kings' men couldn't put Humpty Dumpty back together again". We are like Humpty in that no outside individual or group of well meaning friends can do for us what only a higher power can do for us. Family, friends, co-workers and even strangers cannot put us back together again. They can cheer us on and provide invaluable support. The action must be our own. We can pick up the pieces and start to reassemble what God created.

JULY 7

Responsibility is a key concept in our recovery. We begin by accepting responsibility for the harm we have caused—that is the whole reason for Steps Four and Five. We stop blaming others for the predicaments we found ourselves in. We have a responsibility to be honest first with ourselves and then with those around us. Eventually we are responsible to give back what we have been given. We have a responsibility to help the newcomer by attending meetings, sponsoring them, sharing our stories and we have a responsibility to see that A.A. doesn't founder because of inadequate financial resources.

JULY 8

Wouldn't you want your friends to tell you if you had spinach caught in your front teeth? Then why do we get upset when friends tell us that we are drinking too much? Actually there isn't a good reason to get upset when friends start noticing our drinking is getting out of hand. We should be happy that someone loves us enough to want to keep us from embarrassing ourselves. As noted though, the opposite is often true. The denial that we have a drinking problem is oh so strong because of the misguided notion that alcohol abuse is a moral failing where spinach in the teeth is just a temporary problem requiring little effort to rectify.

JULY 9

A kick in the butt instead of understanding your pain. These are two different approaches to helping the person on the road to recovery. They don't have to be mutually exclusive as each can help the person confront the reality of his situation. Generally though you can attract more bears with honey than with vinegar but nutritionists tell us that there are times when both liquids may be necessary for regaining one's health. What we say or demand of the person will not work if he has not hit bottom and isn't sincere in wanting to change. In any given meeting testimonies in favor of both approaches will be made. The best advice is to know the individual before deciding which approach to use.

JULY 10

The biggest mistake we make is believing that happiness can be found outside ourselves. The story of the Grinch Who Stole Christmas illustrates this principle. The people of Whoville didn't need the gifts under the tree to feel joy and happiness. If you are looking for happiness, visit any town dump and find there the remnants of what was supposed to bring happiness. We only thought the material things would bring us happiness and so we kept desperately seeking happiness in things or more often in our case, the bottle.

JULY 11

The Twelve and Twelve book mentions that nothing much can grow in the dark. There is one thing that does and that is mushrooms. The reality is that mushrooms grow best not only in the dark but in manure. I think that is the kind of growth most of us had once alcohol became the dominant force in our lives. Like the mushrooms, we fed ourselves a daily diet of nutrients that were not conducive to the kind of person we wanted and desired to be. We too were in the dark concerning the effect alcohol was having on our lives and the lives of those around us. Only when we come into the sunshine of the spirit do we want a different diet.

JULY 12

Moby Dick is a story reflective of our dilemma. The Great White Whale could attack from the depths of the ocean while Ahab could only attack from the surface. Our White Whale could attack us from the depths of our souls. Our alcoholism, like Moby Dick with Ahab, has inflicted great pain on us and we have tried to fight it alone. We were limited at first to fighting our whale with our limited personal resources. When we called upon the fellowship of A.A. and our higher power only then could we get to the deepest source of our illness and at least for us to disarm our nemesis. We never really defeat our alcoholism; we only keep it disarmed as long as we are spiritually fit.

JULY 13

Listen at any A.A. meeting and you will find that few of us have an anniversary date of January 1st. I think this is ironic in that I believe that many of us made New Years' Resolutions like almost everyone else. And like everyone else those resolutions didn't last too long. This is true because resolutions are primarily promises to us and good intentions made by the unaided self are seldom fulfilled. New Years' Resolutions are time specific and we can easily succumb to the idea that one more day won't matter. Also contributing to the failure of this resolution is that it is often made with the idea that this is going to be permanent change. What kind of a resolution would it be if it were only for the first day of the New Year? In A.A. we don't promise ourselves to remain sober forever or for the next year. One day at a time works where longer promises often fail.

JULY 14

Why do we lie? Well, we lie to others primarily out of fear but we lie to ourselves for reasons that are different from the lies to others. If we tell a lie often enough we can come to believe it wholeheartedly. The biggest lie we tell ourselves is that we can quit anytime we want to. And then we tell ourselves the lie that we just don't want to. If we have told ourselves the first lie then subconsciously we have admitted that we have a problem otherwise there would be no need to make that first statement. The fact is that few of us can quit on our own volition. So, if you have said, "I can quit anytime I want to", you are lying to yourself.

JULY 15

Why is there such insistence that the ego must be deflated if we are to attain sobriety? The reduction of the ego is the lessening of fear and fear is the great underlying cause of our character defects. We learn that our worth is based on what others think of us—our parents at first and then others as we grow. We fear the rejection and strive to influence the others' thinking. And since our sense of self is based outside ourselves we are under constant pressure to measure up to what we think others want of us. When we reduce dependency on the ego we can truly to learn to love ourselves as ourselves.

JULY 16

Unconditional love is one of the great gifts of membership in A.A. It is not dependent on who we are or what we do or how long we have been sober. Conditional love is dependent on meeting certain restrictions; I love you only if you are sober. Unconditional love does not mean accepting any and all behavior—we do not become doormats in recovery nor should we expect that if you love me you won't condemn my behavior. Love can be demanding–fidelity to truth, to vows made. You can love someone and still not accept bad behavior.

JULY 17

We don't heal a broken leg by numbing it. A doctor would be laughed out of the profession if she just gave you morphine and sent you on your way. Neither can our emotional selves we healed by chemicals although we have tried mightily to do just that. We understand at the basest level that mending the broken leg by setting it and putting in some sort of cast is necessary for our physical bodies. It is also true that our emotional selves must undergo some pain setting right what has been broken and to accept that we must follow some simple casts in the form of rules if we are to truly recover.

JULY 18

Can you imagine stating, "I'm just too busy to shower?" Can you imagine what life would be like for you and those around you? In some ways when we don't pray the results are similar to not taking a shower. Prayer means cleansing ourselves of the debris of the day—the insults given and taken, the quick bursts of anger, the feelings of self-pity, and the disagreements. We amass these emotional feelings many times without even recognizing that they are accumulating. And prayer is useful in reminding ourselves of the beauty that has come our way—the love of our friends, the quick bursts of thanks, and the recognition of progress made and the agreements reached. When you pray imagine what life is like for you and those around you.

JULY 19

"First things first" is one of those simple slogans that are practiced more in saying than in doing. Can you imagine making a list and deciding what has to be done first and then doing the second item first? Does that make sense? Of course it doesn't and yet having attaining sobriety at the top of the list is no guarantee that it remains more important than getting a job, restoring a marriage, apologizing to family and friends or taking a vacation. Newcomers especially have a hard time prioritizing needed actions and that is where a sponsor can be of tremendous help in concentrating on getting sober before anything else. What good will it do to get a job if because of your illness you are likely not to keep it?

JULY 20

"Practicing these principles in all our affairs" is more easily said than done. It is one thing to know what one needs to do and a whole other thing to act on that knowledge. We know from our reading that anger is a "luxury" and yet we find ourselves angry. We know from our reading that forgiveness is necessary but we hang on to hurt feelings. We know that fear is absent of faith, but we succumb to fear. We know we have to face harsh truth, but we hide behind procrastination. Finally we accept that we are truly human and that improvement in all these areas is a steady commitment to trying.

JULY 21

There are days when everything seems to be going wrong: the car won't start, the sink is plugged, the kids are sick and work seems overwhelming. It is then that all that we have heard and spoken should call us into action. We do not live by words but by deeds. Faced with problems, we call for roadside assistance for the car, make a call to the plumber, make arrangements for one parent to stay home and tackle the work one problem at a time. And then we remember that words do help and say the Serenity Prayer.

JULY 22

"Be still and know that I am" are powerful words attributed to a higher power. When we practice those moments of silence in meetings we are setting aside all those notions we have about a higher power and witnessing the strength that comes with humility. Those two descriptive words, "I am" indicate we can know only a little of the great mystery and the admonition to "Be Still" asks us to quiet the raucous thoughts and sounds that barrage us in our daily lives. We know only a little and more will be revealed if we are willing to be still and listen.

JULY 23

It's the beginning of the day and you awake, look around and decide what kind of day you are going to have. What, you may ask? You can either dread what is going to happen or to have joyful expectations. So if you are faced with a stopped sink you can think well I am glad it happened while I could be home and do something about it or you can decide it is all going to go downhill today. Surprisingly, which attitude you take will probably prove to be true for you that day in all your interactions. This doesn't mean life won't happen as it is bound to happen, it does mean you decide how it is going to affect you emotionally. Choose a positive outlook.

JULY 24

It was snowing, cars were in the ditch and a truck had jackknifed. I was driving at 30 miles per hour and it was getting dark. It was only middle October and so we shouldn't be experiencing this kind of weather. I was tense and was really looking forward to getting to our destination. Approaching the resort where we were to stay I suddenly said to my wife, "Wow! You know what would be really good right now?" We can't keep these thoughts from crossing our mind. We can make the right decision, laugh at the absurdity of a drink helping anything and move on. That is what I did.

JULY 25

An old bar that had been closed for several years was undergoing renovation. I commented to my wife that it seemed strange to be adding another sports bar to what would make three of them within half mile of each other. Could they all survive given that several other restaurants serving alcohol were also within walking distance? Then, I remembered when I was drinking in one bar, I was always wondering if the action was someplace else. Having the bars in such close proximity made it easier to keep chasing the elusive desire to be where the excitement was. Never satisfied is a characteristic of the alcoholic.

JULY 26

The recovering alcoholic accepts that disagreements will happen and recognizes that the feelings must be dealt with gently. When we see things differently doesn't mean the other person is right and we are wrong or vice versa. Disagreements do not have to become a source of anger and argument. Acting gently is more than speaking softly; it means avoiding words of judgment and accusation and assigning blame. We do not need to set the other person right or to correct the mistaken views of others. We can say as gently and lovingly as possible, we see things differently.

BILL E.

JULY 27

"Oh no! Not another lesson!" I loved this bumper sticker as it implied frustration that another mistake had been made. "When will I ever learn?" Upon reflection though, I came to understand it in another way. Mistakes are a way to keep me humble and that when I stop learning I may as well be dead. So, I welcome the new lessons and the old ones that are repeated. Few things are learned in life upon the first encounter. It has been written that to be good at something requires a lot of practice—maybe 10,000 times doing it before we get really good at the skill. Lessons repeated and lessons learned once more; thank goodness I am alive to keep having these lessons.

JULY 28

Willingness is the key to recovery. A promise to act better doesn't mean too much unless we ask our higher power for the willingness to have that power make us better. We need to get specific about the kind of actions we need to take to fulfill that promise and then we need the willingness to have the power to do those specific actions. We can promise ourselves and receive the willingness we have prayed for and have identified what we must do but in the end we have to act. The best laid plans are just that, plans. No house appears because an architect has drawn up the design plans. No military operation takes place just because the generals have written a strategic plan. Eventually, builders must be hired and soldiers must move into battle.

JULY 29

"So be good for goodness sake" is a line from a Christmas song that has a potent message about why we should do the right thing. How many of us are truly altruistic or good for goodness sake? Perhaps more than we sometimes recognize. We help another alcoholic because we have been told, and come to realize in time, that in helping the other we are helping ourselves. Is that self-centered thinking? We do not consciously state I'm doing this to help myself. Showing up at a meeting is being good for goodness sake. Our action helps without our immediately knowing that it helps.

JULY 30

When my mother died, I lost more than my mother. Her last years were not good ones for her; a bad heart and a mind that wasn't always coherent. She had thrown away some of the things that were small and I am sure she thought worthless. One of those things was her recipe book with all her handwritten recipes that she had used to cook for her family. Her last years were in a home with my brother and she did no cooking; therefore why keep something so old and now useless? We can't keep everything to pass on, but we should be careful in discarding things personal-her handwritten recipes. For me, my dog-eared Big Book underlined and written in may just be one of those things I'll pass on.

JULY 31

Guilt. Shame. Remorse. Three negative attitudes that we are told we ought to avoid; don't go on a guilt trip. Negative they may be, but we have to hit bottom emotionally as well as physically and these feelings should help us to realize that we have hit bottom. They should prod us to do something to relieve these emotions and that something is the Twelve Steps. After we have worked these Steps we will be able to accept that we were sick when we did the things that brought on guilt, shame and remorse.

AUGUST 1

Revealing our deepest secrets is not for the faint-hearted. It means becoming vulnerable to rejection, scorn and derision. We have to be convinced that the only way forward is to do what is required. It is our ego at its strongest when we balk at sharing these secrets with another person. When we do share, we have to be convinced that the person hearing our revelations will not communicate them to anyone else. A great number of alcoholics share with a priest those secrets and the rest of us will share with our sponsor after we have become convinced that he will honor this sacred trust.

AUGUST 2

Years ago a well known author wrote that he and his family were bound to have to work for a living rather than living off the proceeds from an asset. He had been offered an investment opportunity in a place he saw only as mountainous and rocky and turned down a chance to buy an acre of the land at a $1000 an acre. The area is now known as Aspen, Colorado. We turn down opportunities that could make a difference in our lives. Sadly, too many pass on the opportunity to get sober and remain stuck in a place not of their liking.

AUGUST 3

Author Kinsey Millhome has said that he is in favor of forgiveness as long as he can get even first. I certainly identify with that feeling of wanting to get even for all the harm allegedly done to me. That is the kind of thinking characterized by the old Hatfield and McCoy feuds and for the current conflict between the Israelis and the Palestinians. Letting go of bitterness and feelings of revenge are paths to peace and healing. We can take understanding from the examples of people and nations who cannot forgive but are caught in a never ending spiral of destruction.

AUGUST 4

Ralph Waldo Emerson has written, "Nothing good was ever achieved without enthusiasm." We alcoholics can cheerfully agree with that sentiment. I came into A.A with the belief that the good times were over and that life was going to be all grays and lifeless. As I began to respond to the promises and the examples of happy people in front of me, I too began to grow into enthusiasm for what was possible for me and others. I am enthusiastic in the possibilities of a life without the baleful effects of chemical dependency.

AUGUST 5

A Native American saying states that if there is no wind, row. We cannot get sober just sitting in an A.A. meeting just as we cannot get from the shore merely sitting in a rowboat. There is work to be done and again like the rowboat the effort involved may be hard but it is not complicated. Doing each of the Twelve Steps does not require a PH.D. nor is it rocket science. I am reminded of the ads in my youth for the Arthur Murray Dance Studios where they showed simple box steps indicating how easy it was to learn to dance. The A.A. Twelve Steps are not more complicated than those of Arthur Murray.

AUGUST 6

I'm not young enough to know everything says a lot about the wisdom that can come with age. When we begin drinking at an early age, we essentially stop emotionally maturing. I think this explains why accepting that we know very little when we come into A.A. is so difficult. As men and women grow older their experiences temper their knowledge and we begin to recognize that we know only a little. As alcoholics we stopped growing. In the Big Book we find the statement that more will be revealed. It is those revelations that constitute the wisdom we ask for in the serenity prayer.

AUGUST 7

Much like the walnut that must have its shell cracked and discarded so the good can be utilized, we alcoholics must discard the shell that we have used to keep our god-given goodness hidden. Our shell has been indifference, fear, anger and sloth. The best way to break out of our shell is to allow our friends in A.A. to help us accept the truth about what is causing us so much pain. Our sponsor can play a major role in continually asking what Step we are on and encouraging us to do the next right thing.

BILL E.

AUGUST 8

Know thyself is a well known maxim in A.A. When I came into A.A. I really believed that I knew what was best for me contrary to the overwhelming evidence that the opposite was closer to the truth. Hindsight works wonders when we are asked to seriously look at our past. The Fourth Step asks us to do a moral inventory and it is that inventory when we really begin to look at the person we had become and more importantly what had caused us to end up doing the Fourth Step. When we do subsequent Fourth Steps we are reviewing our core attributes and how well we are doing in that never ending practice of examining who we are.

AUGUST 9

Attempting to rescue a person in danger of drowning is not an easy task. The person needs to relax and trust the person attempting to rescue him. What the drowning person usually does is to fight like hell to stay afloat; it is a natural instinct to stay alive but he is doing the opposite of what he needs to do: that is to let go and let the person take him to safety. Alcoholics are like the drowning person. In fighting our disease we fight like the devil against the person who may lead us to safety. This is the lesson we need to learn: to let go and let God in the form of an A.A. member.

AUGUST 10

The A.A. slogans are often dismissed in early sobriety as being rather simplistic. And they are. So, when we say that this is a simple program we have the slogans in mind. But simple and simplistic are not necessarily bad because they do help us focus on what is necessary for sobriety. We need to make sure that the slogans do not just remain on the walls where we meet, but are put to memory to be called on when faced with the inevitable decisions that can affect our sobriety. Easy does it can help us remember that we do not need to expect instant changes in our ability to handle anger.

AUGUST 11

If we are watching television and we do not like what we are seeing, we change channels. We can apply that principle to our everyday lives: We can leave an uncomfortable situation or we can change our attitude about that situation. We are not hopeless nor are we incapacitated. It may take more than what is required to change a TV channel by pressing a button but we are increasingly in charge of those things we can change as asked for in the Serenity Prayer. Sloth is one of the seven deadly sins and we can take action.

BILL E.

AUGUST 12

During winter in the part of the country that I live in, we can experience an unexpected bout of good weather: the sky is clear and the temperature is above normal. The common refrain among the residents is that "we will pay for this later". We don't fully enjoy the moment because of dread that this period of good weather will inevitably be followed by a really harsh blast of cold and snow. How often are other parts of our lives like this? We project that while things are pretty good right now, the future looks bleak. Remember to enjoy the good.

AUGUST 13

Albert Einstein is quoted as saying that,"We can't solve problems by using the same kind of thinking we used when we created them". There are two gems to get from that quotation for us alcoholics: our old ways of thinking didn't work for us and our problems are of our own making. If we are to get and remain sober we are going to have to change our way of thinking. How do we do that? We change our pattern of thinking. For instance if we think that shit happens we can change that to good happens. We look for substantiation of good happening. But before we can change our thinking we have to do the First Step: recognize we have a problem.

AUGUST 14

While many of us struggle with doing the Fourth Step we should keep in mind that if we are married our spouses could probably complete the Step for us in record time. Those of us not married probably have a relative or friend who could do the same. As alcoholics we are the last to see our defects. We do not have the ability to see ourselves as our partners, friends and relatives do. This is why doing the Ninth Step is so difficult—it is admitting to those who know us best what they already know and have experienced with us.

AUGUST 15

Even with several years in A.A. I still exhibit character defects that brought me so much anguish while drinking. I had a real angry exchange with my wife after she accused me of not fulfilling a promise she was sure I had made. I had not made such a promise and her accusation caused me to say inappropriate words and to storm out of the room. A few minutes later, recognizing that my behavior was wrong I admitted as such. I had not made the promise and I was correct about that, but it was my reaction that was wrong. That is what I apologized for and needed to do. We can be right and still be wrong just as I was in that heated exchange.

AUGUST 16

When we have lived enough and made enough mistakes we are justifiably embarrassed by how carelessly we have lived. When we recognize what we have done and are more than embarrassed we are moved to do something to end the embarrassment. Or we continue to avoid facing the consequences of our behavior by drowning it in booze. The latter decision leads to complete demoralization mentioned in the Big Book. The former decision leads to serenity and peace. The choices couldn't be clearer.

AUGUST 17

There comes a time in every A.A. member's life when having practiced the Twelve Steps we experience a connection to fellow sufferers of this disease and to a higher power. This is when we know in the depths of our very being that we are linked in a web of life that is powered by love. We will have twinges of regret that it took us so long to get to this understanding but we need to accept that it's okay because we get it now. We can fully live saddened only by those who were offered this life-affirming reality and who for reasons not knowable died an alcoholic death.

AUGUST 18

Cinderella had every reason to be angry at her stepmother and stepsisters. I suppose she could have run after their carriage shouting obscenities. In addition to the foul language she would surely have been justified in the eyes of alcoholics of planning revenge on them. There is such a thing as justified anger and in the case of this well known tale we can see it quite clearly. But anger expressed in language or action would not have altered the stepmother and stepsisters. We can't expect a fairy godmother to change things for us as she did for Cinderella. The changes must be of our own doing.

AUGUST 19

A nephew of mine was once in a foot race with friends and quickly realizing that he was not going to win yelled out before the finish line was crossed, "Not included!" He believed that he had saved himself from losing in a competitive race. This is acceptable behavior if you are a child but how many of us because of our drinking backed out of competitive situations preferring the safe confines of a bar. "I could've won", may salve our feelings at the time but we lost out on a lot of good things because we preferred drinking rather than running the race of life.

AUGUST 20

Escape is no longer a choice for recovering alcoholics. We spent a lot of time and resources trying to avoid the normal ups and downs of life and building life-affirming relationships. The bottle gave temporary relief from the fears that punctuated our existence. And because the relief was temporary we were doomed to continue the unrelenting cycle of fear followed by bouts of drinking leading to more fear when we began to dry out. The failed relationships were followed by more failed relationships. Only when we accept that fear was the driving force in our lives could we begin to halt the destructive patterns that shaped us.

AUGUST 21

There is both good and bad in all of us. The inventory we do should illustrate this. There is a very good metaphor used to illustrate this by comparing our good and bad selves to a wolf. The bad wolf is filled with anger, envy, greed, self-pity, lies and false pride while the good wolf is filled with joy, peace, serenity, humility and love. Which of these wolves win? The answer is the one you feed the most. Prior to our coming into A.A. we fed one of these wolves and starved the other. Today, hopefully the good wolf gets our attention and feeding.

AUGUST 22

The critics of a movie entitled Master of Disguise claimed how could you not enjoy the stupidity of the characters? That's what we A.A.'s do with each other now that we have recovered from our hopelessness. We wrote the script and performed as the main character in what could probably be described as a tragic-comedy. A.A. meetings are filled with laughter as we recount our stories. Our lives certainly had both elements where in retrospect our behavior could be seen as clownish at best and tragic at worst. When we make these observations for the first time we are ready to admit our shortcomings.

AUGUST 23

In Genesis we read that God was pleased with what he created. After each new creation he exclaimed, "This is good". If good was good enough for God then good is good enough for us. I also like to believe that after the creative acts he set about to improve them through evolution. For few of us, including God, first attempts lead to what we want for the final product. We continue to grow and change and to respond to what we learn and experience. Before coming into A.A. we were engaged in a destructive pattern of being stuck in behavior that no longer worked. We had to change in order to live.

AUGUST 24

Humility is an often misunderstood concept. There is a perhaps apocryphal story of Don Schula and his family of six entering a theater and the few people in attendance rose and clapped. After the movie ended he said to one of the other individuals leaving that he was pleased that they welcomed him with applause. The person said, "Oh the theater owner said he wouldn't start the movie until at least six more people came. We were applauding that the number had been reached". We are like that. We suddenly realize that the world is not always responding to our personal attributes. That is when we begin to gain humility.

AUGUST 25

There is little doubt that much of the success of A.A. comes directly from the efforts of the two founders. We need to remember though that they were men much like ourselves with all the human limitations. There is a danger that they will be elevated to saint status when it is claimed that the Big Book was divinely inspired. Let's keep the human in this endeavor. Bill and Bob were deeply suspicious of making them larger than life as demonstrated by their desire to be buried quietly and privately. We need not make them larger than life because of their special ability to recognize what could work in their personal lives could also help countless others. That is their legacy to us.

AUGUST 26

One person talking to another person is such a simple concept about how to change behavior. Perhaps it is hard to accept that this works because of entrenched interests who are invested in different expensive approaches. There is a growing body of evidence that this approach may also work in areas of human behavior not even imagined just a short time ago. Violent behavior can apparently be dramatically reduced when one person talks to another person about that behavior especially when it comes from an individual who had engaged in violent behavior. What Bill and Bob discovered about alcoholics may also work to reduce violent crime in America.

AUGUST 27

A definition of hell applies to us alcoholics: I'm here at this place and wish I weren't. We were constantly agitated (non-acceptance) about the inevitable. In our case the inevitable was that we were stuck between the agony of drinking that no longer worked and the need to drink. The same feelings happen in our first attempts at getting sober. We have a desire to leave A.A. by pretending that the problem either doesn't exist or is a minor problem. Until we quit fighting the unavoidable reality that we can no longer drink socially, if we ever could, we will be living in hell.

AUGUST 28

The movie, Pretty Woman, made prostitution look glamorous and sophisticated. The same can be true about alcohol use at least for us alcoholics. We are prone to think of the enticing aspects of alcohol especially when the use requires some special knowledge about the wine or mixed drink. We are likely to think of the dark mahogany wood of the neighborhood bar with its sparkling liquors highlighted by soft lighting and forget what happens to us after indulging in those liquors. Looking glamorous and sophisticated is not the same as glamorous and sophisticated. A campaign slogan of a few years ago sums up our alcohol use," it's like putting lipstick on a pig."

AUGUST 29

The statement, "I will not let some minor problem, the breaking of a shoelace for example, cause me to go back to drinking" carries some degree of danger. It implies that some major problem might cause me to pick up a drink to compensate for the problem. We need to remind ourselves that there is no reason, good, bad, large, small, or in-between, that will be adequate for creating the craving and compulsion that follows from taking a drink. Nothing caused us to drink in the past; nothing can cause us to drink now or in the future.

AUGUST 30

I have often said that sobriety is a gift. If so, it is a strange gift in that in order to receive the gift you must put in a lot of effort. To continue receiving the gift you must persist in making an effort to keep it. I now try to think of sobriety as a talent that one has developed. One can be able to sing, for example, but unless you put in an effort you will never really become good at it. Or you can have a talent for a particular sport, but unless you practice and make some major commitment to the game you will not get good at it. I believe every person has a talent for staying sober, but that few are willing to put in the time and work to make it happen for them.

SEPTEMBER 1

Why did so many of us dismiss the danger we were facing with our continued use of alcohol? Why do people take risks that are out of proportion to any value gained? We could not function if we had to stop and weigh every decision as to its possible danger. If we have avoided past bad consequences under similar circumstances we are even less likely to take notices of small changes in those circumstances. When we drive drunk and get away with it, we see less danger of getting caught the next time we have drunk too much and decide to drive. Newspapers and television stories are full of the consequences of drinking and driving. It happens to us.

SEPTEMBER 2

We are neither a mistake nor a problem to be solved. We are human beings who fall short of what we could be. No person operates at a full level of competence in all areas of life. None of us is good at everything. That said we are also capable of being more than we currently are. We need to accept that having the potential to lead a sober life doesn't mean that we will. Sobriety is more than not drinking. It is acting in a way that benefits those around us and far from us. Spirituality can be seen as acting in the best interest of the interdependent web of life.

SEPTEMBER 3

I needed to come to the understanding that I didn't want the alcohol; I wanted the way alcohol made me feel: funny, good-looking, in charge of my life. Eventually what happened was alcohol no longer worked to make me funny, good-looking and in charge of my life. I kept chasing those now elusive feelings hoping without reason to recapture again what alcohol had once done for me. Sometimes I would get close to those feelings but because of the nature of my disease I kept drinking to the point that those feelings were quickly dissipated. Finding new ways to feeling good about me is necessary for continued sobriety. I also needed to change what made me feel good about me from a focus on me to a focus on helping others.

SEPTEMBER 4

Those who study human nature have concluded that belief comes first followed by facts. What this means is that we find the facts that buttress our beliefs. When we started drinking we believed that it would provide us with something we were perhaps unknowingly wanting. We drank and the results were seen as positive even though we may have gotten terribly sick. The costs didn't happen right away or they were ignored. We focused on the good—the facts that would convince us that using alcohol was a good thing. We had fun, we enjoyed being with others and those became the facts we accepted.

SEPTEMBER 5

Forgiving those who have harmed us is never explicitly listed as something we should do. The Lord's Prayer recited at many meetings asks God to forgive us as we forgive others. Real or imagined hurts still need to be forgiven. Whatever our role may or may not have been in these situations, others are often just as sick as we were. It is in forgiving that we heal ourselves; carrying resentments, whoever was at fault, is deadly. Forgiving asks a lot of us but no one said that getting and remaining sober was going to be easy. We also need to be careful that the act of forgiving is not something we can take satisfaction in as forgiving is primarily for our own benefit.

SEPTEMBER 6

Exaggeration is a character defect closely allied with our ego. Our exploits while drinking were often a source of demented pride: "you really made an ass of yourself last night!" gave us a sense of being unique in our early drinking careers. We, along with our friends, laughed the behavior off as a price to pay for belonging to the group. We have to be on guard against such misplaced pride when telling our stories. Is the story we tell a true one that brings laughter or is it primarily one that encourages feeling of self-importance?

SEPTEMBER 7

The road to hell is paved with good intentions. The road back from hell is also paved with good intentions. Good intentions are similar to the decision we make in Step Three. And like Step Three we have to do the follow up work that such a decision or intention requires of us. We intended to have only two drinks, to leave the bar in an hour, to get to the kids baseball game and we intended to stay away from the drink the next day. Those intentions often led to failure. Today our intention to get sober requires us to do the action required in Steps Four through Nine. Good intentions we know only too well are not enough.

SEPTEMBER 8

We have a convoluted relationship with some of the A.A. slogans. Take for example the suggestion to "Think, Think, Think." When we also hear that, "Your best thinking got you where you are today", we pretend to be confused: Should we think or not think? As with other aspects of the program, we need to quit arguing with ourselves over multiple meanings and accept that recovery means thinking before acting. The thinking we did prior to coming into A.A. was that we acted before thinking and we know how that practice worked out for us.

SEPTEMBER 9

"The chimes of time ring out the news another day is through. Someone slipped and fell, was that someone you?" are words found in a popular hymn. Those words have great meaning for us. We may not have slipped as alcoholics use the word. But all of us have slipped in what we hope to be and do. In the Tenth Step we identify where we have slipped in our relationship to those family, friends, acquaintances and passersby as each day passes. Slipping is normal and making immediate amends is just as normal.

SEPTEMBER 10

In to every life some rain must fall. Think of that statement. It implies that rain is negative. Yet life cannot exist without rain. The same can be said of pain. Pain is a positive thing. Empathy comes from our experiencing pain and loss. We couldn't really be alive without experiencing pain. Pain should be welcome for what it teaches us. The Buddha left his sheltered life and lived among the poor explaining what it meant to live that way. "I'm awake". What can I learn from this painful experience that will help me become a better person; to be awake is to experience life both positive and painful.

SEPTEMBER 11

Alcoholics tend to believe that if they can restrict the amount of alcohol they consume, they will be able to drink sensibly since they see so many other people drinking sensibly. Aren't I just as good as the person who stops at two? This isn't a question of good and bad but how alcoholic bodies for whatever reasons are not like the non-alcoholic bodies. Some people can't consume peanuts, we can't consume alcohol. Trying to stop drinking is often a pre-requisite to stopping.

SEPTEMBER 12

Sometimes in meetings I hear that the person is not going to tell his story because he wants to focus on how he is staying sober. Well, I disagree. Telling our story keeps it fresh in our mind which has a tendency to focus on the good in our lives and not the bad. When we tell our stories we are less prone to believe the falsehood that it wasn't so bad or to blame others. History is replete with stories of people and nations not remembering what got them where they are.

SEPTEMBER 13

Physical therapists have made a rather interesting discovery: slow workouts burn more fat than fast workouts. This is the opposite of what most people try to do when first going on a new workout routine; they want to do the physical activities at a high rate of speed primarily because they believe they can make up for the time they haven't been exercising. I think the findings about burning fat apply to our alcoholism. I have heard it said in many meetings that slow growth is good growth. The victory doesn't come to those who are the quickest but the most persistent.

SEPTEMBER 14

Anything we try to do to improve our physical, mental and social health is easier if we stay focused. Those of us who have tried meditation for example often give up because it is too hard to stay focused on the present. Every individual who meditates knows of the difficulty in quieting the mind. Mundane thoughts constantly interrupt the attempt at meditating. Those of us who attempt to improve our mental acuity often quit after a few times at doing the mental exercises or doing the required reading and contemplation about the subject matter. If we are to stay sober we have to stay focused on the behaviors that will help us succeed at sobriety: the behaviors outlined in the Twelve Steps of Alcoholics Anonymous.

SEPTEMBER 15

Interesting data about worry and fear has been discovered. Sixty percent of our fears never come to pass, twenty percent are about the past that we can do nothing about, ten percent are so trivial as to not warrant our attention leaving about ten percent of which only four or five percent are fears that are truly justified. So, if these figures are correct, we spend ninety-five percent as totally wasted time worrying. So we can't say with absolute certainty to be happy don't worry but it makes a lot of sense.

SEPTEMBER 16

Why did most ancient cultures revere the elders of their tribe or clan? They possessed the accumulated wisdom of years of experience and learning. They had learned not to judge too harshly and to forgive trespasses. The old-timers in A.A. are of a similar bent. They know only too well that the program works because it is based on suggestions rather than coercion. The word education comes from a Latin word meaning to draw out. That is the basis of A.A., to educate and to draw out from the newcomer what they already know about why their behavior has brought them to where they are today.

SEPTEMBER 17

Albert Einstein insisted that there were only two ways to live: as if everything was a miracle or as if nothing was a miracle. What does that mean? If you look at the heavens through the modern telescopes you see how remarkable it is that life exists on this planet at all. Life as we know it is not common in all the galaxies then it can be justly said that it is a miracle that we are here at all. A miracle is defined as contrary to what could be expected. Given the history of our drinking and the history of alcohol use and abuse by individuals throughout world history, then our sobriety can truly be called miraculous.

SEPTEMBER 18

There are those who call the program of Alcoholics Anonymous selfish. It isn't. It is a program of self-interest and there is a world of difference in those similar terms. It is in our self-interest to practice the principles of A.A. and to focus on our recovery. Selfish would mean that we would not want to share the advantages of sobriety with others and that would not be in our self-interest. If we do not focus on doing what is required to stay sober even when it asks us to spend less time with our family, we are not focusing on our self-interest. If we do not stay alive, we can't be of help.

SEPTEMBER 19

Do not guess what others mean or guess what their body language may or may not be saying. One characteristic of people under the influence of alcohol is that they have restricted ability to make accurate interpretations of words or actions of others. We have to learn how to ask what a person is saying, to ask for clarification. We also owe it to others to state explicitly what we want and need. How many times did I say, she ought to know what I needed without me asking. How ridiculous does that look on the printed page? And when I did that I could assume a superior position of how little the person cares for me when she doesn't act without my having to ask. I think the term in these cases is called being on a pity pot.

SEPTEMBER 20

Don't believe everything you think is good advice. The great advances in scientific endeavors have been because of the practice of peer review. When scientists believe they have made a discovery or have uncovered new facts that support a previous discovery, they ask fellow scientists in their field to review their work. All of us have ideas that need to be subject to review by people who have accepted credentials in the specialty. Members both old and new depend on our own kind of "peer review" to keep us well grounded and save us from acting without good reasons for doing so. That is fundamentally the answer to why A.A. works: peer review-one alcoholic talking to another alcoholic.

SEPTEMBER 21

"But, I don't want to go among mad people", Alice remarked.

"Oh, you can help that", said the Cat. "We're all mad here. I'm mad, you're mad".

"How do you know I'm mad", asked Alice.

"You must be." said the Cat. Or you wouldn't be here."

From time to time someone will come into an A.A. meeting wondering if they are an alcoholic or not. And, like the Cat in Alice in Wonderland, members reply, "You must be or you wouldn't be here". People who are not alcoholic never wonder if they are addicted to alcohol or not.

SEPTEMBER 22

New scientific findings indicate that how we behave influences how others behave and how they behave influences us. We may not have had the scientific research to back the statement up, but we know from personal experiences how valid the findings are. When we drank we sought out people who drank like us and acted accordingly. Now that we attend A.A. meetings and hang with people who are sober our behavior is like those around us. This is the power of the fellowship of A.A. and what we mean when we say that we are not alone.

SEPTEMBER 23

I certainly wished at the beginning of my sobriety that the Serenity Prayer had said courage to change people instead of things. There were lots of people who needed changing and still do. The realization that my ability to change them is almost nil was the beginning of sanity. I believe that If only, and fill in the person's name here, would do what I wanted or desisted in doing what the person was doing I wouldn't act the way I did or feel the way I felt. When my happiness depended on what the other person did or didn't do, then I was a slave to that person. In sobriety I threw off the shackles of slavery.

SEPTEMBER 24

Calm deliberation was not my approach to situations that bothered me. Anger, resentment, and self-pity were my usual responses. Anger made me feel in control: My anger showed how seriously I took the offending behavior of the other; resentment gave me a sense of the superiority of my position: self-pity offered me the hope that others would recognize how much they hurt me and would out of a sense of guilt, do what I wanted. How sick were those feelings and rationalizations? I can recognize my insanity today. Today I try to remain calm through the use of any of the prayers in the Big Book and pray that I will accept that which I may not like.

SEPTEMBER 25

When I began my morning run one cold winter morning it wasn't snowing, but in a short time the snow began to fall and I was more than half way through the run. I really thought that my wife would see the snow and would come in the car and pick me up. She didn't and when I got in the house I stormed, "Didn't you see the snow and didn't you think I would like for you to pick me up? She replied, "No, I didn't". Well, I was deflated. I always assumed that everybody, especially my wife, would know what I needed. In sobriety I have learned not to expect others to intuitively know what I need. I am not the center of the universe. I need to learn to ask for what I want.

SEPTEMBER 26

Oh, how I loved to identify the mistakes and errors of others. If I couldn't meet the achievements of others, I could at least spot the failings of my co-workers. And it is rather easy to do so since very few people lead lives of exemplary behavior in all their activities. Or, I could identify how their achievements were not the result of their work, but of fortunate circumstances unavailable to me. It is that unwillingness to judge others by the same standard that I used to judge my behavior that is one of my shortcomings. I am always more willing to excuse my own defects than I am to extend the same willingness to those around me and conversely my successes were always the result of my special qualities.

SEPTEMBER 27

We would consider someone a little off base if he walked into a room and stumbled in the dark while unwilling to turn on a light switch. We would be even more incredulous if that person repeated that behavior. Most of us would say to that person, "for god's sake turn on the light". Yet, we continue similar behavior in our personal lives. We repeat behavior that on reflection makes no sense whatsoever. We continue to drink and drive, even in many cases, when we have faced arrests and huge financial costs. Most people would say to us, "for god's sake quit drinking and driving, better yet quit drinking."

SEPTEMBER 28

"What shall I do?" is a question that I learned to ask in A.A. meetings. Relying solely on my own thinking led me invariably to dissatisfaction with the outcome. No person can possible know how to successfully handle every situation faced in life. We study history in school to learn what has failed and what has succeeded. We study the lives of men and women for insight into our own behavior. We listen to others in A.A. meetings to learn how they handled similar troubles. It has been said that we do not have to re-invent the wheel. We don't have to find on our own resources what works and doesn't work. A.A. meetings are really meetings of amateur historians reporting on their own research.

SEPTEMBER 29

Studies of human behavior are fascinating. It is known that people associate qualities they say about other people with their own qualities. That is if you call someone warm and thoughtful, those who hear you state this about another person, they assume that you have those qualities! Conversely, if you call that someone a cheat and a thief, you're seen as being like that. Think of that! There is another element in that finding: if you think of yourself as a failure or any other negative quality, you are more likely to see that in others. It has been said that sticks and stones may break my bones, but words can really harm me is true in so many ways.

SEPTEMBER 30

If your only tool is a hammer, then everything looks like a nail is a good metaphor for tapping into the assorted tools offered through the program of Alcoholics Anonymous. Prayer can be an effective tool, but not if it is used to avoid doing the things required to tackle the problem. Asking for help from an alcoholic can be helpful but not if it is used to avoid doing what is apparent that should be done. Asking forgiveness can be helpful but not if it is used to escape the consequences of our actions. Admission of our defects is good, but not if it relieves us to take action with all due speed. We may not always know what tool to use, but we can practice using all the tools and finding out what works.

OCTOBER 1

People behave better when a mirror is present and they behave even better when pictures of eyes are on the walls. Apparently we don't like to see ourselves behaving badly and as long as we don't see ourselves literally or figuratively, we are more likely to act badly. And if we think we are being watched in either of these two ways we behave better than we would without the eyes or mirrors. Robert Burns has written, "Oh, the gift the giftie could give us, to see ourselves as others see us". This judgment ought to cause us to mentally keep in mind how we appear to others. Would your parents be proud of what you're doing is still a good standard to think about and use.

OCTOBER 2

There is no requirement in sobriety to lose your right to object to treatment by others. If you act like a doormat you will be treated like a doormat and there is no need to be treated that way. How we object is important. I often reacted inappropriately when I was drinking—with anger or even worse, rage. At times I acted with exaggerated hurt feelings in an often forlorn hope it would cause others to feel sorry for me and change their actions. Simply stating that I object to your treating me that way because it diminishes my sense of self-worth is a much better way than yelling "you're an idiot" or some other epithet. Learning how to be calm in chaotic situations is a much needed attribute.

OCTOBER 3

Nutritionists describe what has been called the fat trap. It is extremely difficult to lose weight because the cells in our body react during the dieting as if they are starving. When the dieter begins eating again the cells start storing the calories and the dieter gains back the weight he lost. This may also explain the phenomenon that happens after individuals go back drinking after a period of sobriety. It has been noted that the individual who resumes drinking is right back where he left off. Our cells may be hungry for the alcohol like the cells of fat people desire calories. Unlike overweight people who do have to eat, alcoholics are fortunate in that we do not have to drink alcohol.

OCTOBER 4

When medical doctors prescribe medicine, they find that many stop taking the medicine when they begin to feel better rather than taking the complete prescription. This often leads to the illness coming back even stronger because the viruses causing the illness have evolved into a stronger strain. The same can be said for alcoholics who stop doing what they should do to keep alcoholism in remission. After my first treatment and being sober for a couple of months I mistook my feeling better as proof that I wasn't an alcoholic. This scenario is repeated over and over again with the result that the disease comes back often stronger than when first treated.

OCTOBER 5

During the autumn months critters from the outside start coming into houses for warmth and food. If you aren't aggressive in getting at the first mouse you see, you're going to have a real problem with mice rather shortly. I think this is true for alcohol: we take one drink and before we comprehend what is happening, we are having a real problem with alcohol once again. As in the case of mice or other critters invading our homes, we have to be vigilant in avoiding the often small seemingly unimportant fissures that can cause alcohol to run rampant in our lives. "What can go wrong if I miss talking with my sponsor", is one of those fissures.

OCTOBER 6

I doubt if any alcoholic faced with the realization that he is powerless against alcohol has ever said, "Well, I can hardly wait for someone to tell me what to do". Almost to a person we have believed that we were in control and that we could handle whatever life threw at us. And in many situations that might very well have been true. Many of us in our professional lives are quite competent and excellent leaders. But when it comes to alcohol, we have to admit that with alcohol we are faced with something that confounds us and has us in its grip. The belief that we can handle anything is challenged when we are told that we have to take directions from someone we may not know. Our initial reaction is to resist. Only when that resistance is overcome will we be able to get and stay sober.

OCTOBER 7

Will power is a strange human characteristic. In many if not all other ways alcoholics can exert will power to change behaviors that are destructive or damaging. I did quit smoking entirely on my own through grit and determination. I had tried limiting the amount of cigarettes I would smoke in an hour and that didn't work. I tried not buying a pack and bumming off friends. Finally, with the birth of my first son, I made the decision to quit and did so. With alcohol my will power was non-existent. I tried similar approaches to those I tried with smoking and none worked. I tried cold turkey and that didn't work. Only when I followed the recommendations made in the Big Book did I succeed in eliminating the obsession with alcohol.

OCTOBER 8

There is a widely seen ad for a drug called Abilify that will keep depression under control. The picture shows depression always hanging around the cartoon character ready to come back in full force. Where ever the character is, depression is there in the background. That's a lot like alcoholism. For most of us it is in remission, but we are never cured and it can come roaring back into our lives. We have seen it happen thousands of times as recovering alcoholics do not take the alcohol treatment seriously and succumb once again to the debilitating effects of alcoholism. Some of us continue to wish that science could produce something like Abilify for alcoholism. I suspect that alcoholism will not so easily be defeated.

OCTOBER 9

Interesting how so many alcoholics have a difficult time differentiating hurt from help. Before we come into recovery we accused those who are telling us that we might be drinking too much or that we are making fools of ourselves much too often, as trying to hurt us rather than help us. Part of our sickness is that we cannot often tell the true from the false. We think they are either jealous of our ability to have a good time or that they unable to enjoy themselves. And so we resent and ultimately reject not only the statements but avoid those who don't really understand us. We become increasingly isolated from those who can see so clearly what we cannot see at all.

OCTOBER 10

It helps if family and friends are supportive of the person's desire to get sober. But, and this is a big but, it is not necessary to getting and staying sober. Too often we have used as an excuse that family and friends caused us to drink. If friends and family are still using and discouraging you from sobriety, it is difficult to ignore or reject their opposition. That is why lots of meetings and having a sponsor often proves essential in any one's attempt to do the right thing and change the destructive patterns of behavior. It may mean having to separate from loved ones, at least for a time, and that gives meaning to the phrase going to any length to stay sober.

OCTOBER 11

Body armor protects the body but it also contains and any further growth is very limited. So it is with the shell we hide behind with our fears, anxiety, anger and resentments. When we gradually release ourselves through working through the Twelve Steps, we experience great emotional and mental growth. This growth is thought to occur naturally and for most it does unless that growth is interrupted. Alcohol interrupts that emotional growth and the individual continues to act in ways appropriate for a child but not as an adult. Can any of us suffering from alcoholism deny that our actions were often inappropriate for an adult?

OCTOBER 12

There is no diploma awarded for learning how to live life on life's terms. For whether or not we are alcoholic everyone continues learning how to be fully human. The human needs for safety, love, esteem and self-actualization have been well established by psychologists. For every one of those needs, we have found ourselves wanting. When we do the Fourth Step we find out how each of our resentments was fueled by our own fears about safety and our need for love. We learn how our esteem was affected with each person and place that we found on our list. In all cases, we learned how we fueled those resentments.

OCTOBER 13

Pride is one of the seven deadly sins and the source of many of our character defects. Pride keeps us from admitting that we are powerless over alcohol and is an obstacle to all the other Steps. It is often a subtle shortcoming that is too easily ignored. Justified pride may be as dangerous as justified anger. Recovering alcoholics must attend to the danger of pride in being sober. Praise one can get from fellow recovering alcoholics can lead to false pride. I have been told a number of times that the length of sobriety I have is awesome. That can quickly morph into a belief that I am awesome forgetting the help that made that time possible.

OCTOBER 14

"Having had a spiritual awakening" is an interesting phrase as part of the Twelfth Step. Just what is that awakening? If self-centeredness is the major fault line for our illness, then it seems apparent that we would awaken from that emphasis on self to a growing awareness of those around us. And that I think is what happens. We become less interested in our needs, desires and wants to a position of being concerned with what our family, friends and co-workers need. We begin to want to serve others, to help them. Sometimes we are awakened in real life by the sound of an alarm clock or sometimes we gradually awaken to the sights and sounds around us. Living a sober life is like that: sometimes we can see the immediate need to help another person. Other times we slowly begin to recognize that we are not the center of the universe.

OCTOBER 15

Recovery is not an event, but a process. We may have recovered from the most immediate aspects of our illness, but we go on with our need to maintain the new ways of behaving and thinking. No one can attain perfection, nor is it a reasonable goal. Each day we meet the challenges, frustrations, ignorance, pettiness and ugliness of a life lived and meet the successes, victories, intelligence, significant and beauty of life with similar acceptance. Our lives have become balanced no matter what life throws at us; we remain grounded in the principles of a life better understood. People celebrate the complete remission of physical diseases, we make note that alcoholism is only in abeyance.

OCTOBER 16

Feelings aren't facts but they are real. As a retired college professor I relied on reason, skepticism and logic. Nothing wrong with those attributes; they have helped us create a civilization that has made life good for a great number of people. There are other ways of knowing—emotion, intuition, trust. In A.A. we say that we need to get in touch with our feelings but not let them control us either. When drinking our emotions were often in control which meant paradoxically that our life was out of control. Anger, self-pity, remorse, resentments, guilt needed to be replaced with the emotions of calmness, acceptance, love, empathy and respect to name a few. That is the growth we engage in as we work the steps of A.A.

OCTOBER 17

Surrender and resignation have similar definitions. Surrender is where you quit with hope that you will stay alive. Resignation is staying alive with no hope. The first takes courage. The second lacks faith. When you surrender you quit in order to stay alive. The phrase connotes acceptance that the person has no chance of winning whether on the battlefield or with personal demons. When one surrenders that person stays alive and therefore the possibility increases dramatically that the end result will be good. Not guaranteed mind you, but chances are better than dead. Resignation lacks hope for a better future and seems bleak indeed. With alcohol I surrendered but did not resign. A.A. promises we will have" a new peace and a new happiness". Surrender is necessary, resignation is not.

OCTOBER 18

Television news has the practice of scrolling news across the bottom of the screen while reporting on other stories. I find that distracting: reading the news item distracts me from listening and watching the regular scheduled news or I catch only a few words on the scroll and then wonder what I missed. I think my drinking was like that. While I was acting out I had that "scroll" going through my head asking whether the people liked me, whether I was part of what was going on or rebuking myself for some failing. Life was becoming a distraction. Focusing on the moment and on what is readily apparent helps keep me on the right path.

OCTOBER 19

Anonymity is increasingly difficult to maintain. It is the spiritual foundation of A.A. and it is being threatened by the new means of communication. Going to A.A. websites leaves a permanent record. Receiving uplifting messages from a number of sources including some well known rehab groups leaves an imprint. Emailing friends and about what has been experienced with another alcoholic is similarly recorded. All of this leaves a trail. If others find out that I'm an alcoholic, that is not a source of shame nor is it breaking anonymity. Personal anonymity today means ,as I suspect it did when A.A. was founded ,is that I do not deliberately set out to let the public at large know that I'm in A.A. It is the self-aggrandizement that is dangerous for my sobriety and for all other parts of my life.

OCTOBER 20

Old timers, and there is no agreed upon definition of such, are sometimes given too much reverence, after all they are or were recovering alcoholics. The older timers seem to have had some great insight and ability to act in just the right approach to helping alcoholics according to the praise heaped upon them. They didn't coddle any newcomer as we who are in A.A. today are accused of doing. Yet if you go back to some of the early Grapevine articles you will read the same lamentations then as we hear now: A.A. is not the same as it was and is somehow lesser than our forbearers. Even in the early years there were fears that A.A. was becoming too soft. We simply do not know what will work for every individual—some of us need a strong disciplinary approach and others need gentle guidance into accepting the principles of A.A. One size doesn't fit all.

OCTOBER 21

The lyrics of a popular song say that we can get by with a little help from our friends. In A.A. we need more than a little help from our friends, we need help even from people who aren't necessarily our friends. It has been said that we don't have to like everyone in A.A. but we damn well better love them. That seeming contradiction is only one of many in A.A. What does this one mean? No one can like every one given the personalities and backgrounds of the membership. We ought to love what they are doing for themselves and for us and for the countless others that they no longer are harming. Who couldn't love a person who no longer is a threat on the road or in the home and who are in fact making life better for those around them?

OCTOBER 22

Being able to quote from the book from memory including the page number is impressive, or at least it is to me. It demonstrates a commitment to reading the Big Book and to implementing the principles, suggestions and directions that is commendable. More important though than memorizing passages from the Big Book is living those principles. Quoting verbatim from the Big Book is no guarantee of maintaining one's sobriety. One can know the words to a song and not know the melody and I think that may true of those who memorize the Big Book. It may also illustrate the character defect of self-centeredness. What is the motive behind the memorization? Is it to show one's superior ability or to help remember what action needs to be taken?

OCTOBER 23

The current political climate is marked by rabid accusations and thoughtless charges of disloyalty and in many ways it seems more so than in other times. Thank the founders of A.A. who were wise enough to state that A.A. has no opinion on outside issues. In any AA meeting we do note that people with widely divergent view in politics, religion, vegetarianism, sexual orientation and a host of other issues can meet to solve their common problem of alcoholism. Many say that the country would be better off if more people followed the principles of A.A. Acceptance of others whatever their background is a wonderful principle. I can only add an Amen.

OCTOBER 24

A.A. literature speaks of the Seven Deadly Sins: Pride, Anger, Greed, Gluttony, Lust, Envy and Sloth. In recovery we can focus on the virtues that are opposite of those sins: Humility, patience, charity, temperance, chastity, patience and diligence. At first glance we might want to exhibit those virtues. An example of this is the danger of someone who was a spendthrift suddenly becomes a miser. Being generous to a suffering alcoholic seems like a good idea unless it means, as Bill W. pointed out, that members of his family would have to do without. I get a large number of appeals for monetary donations and all of them are worthy of my support. If it means those I love do without, it is not a virtue. If taken to extremes even virtues are not virtues and may reflect a psychological need for acceptance that is not mentally healthy.

OCTOBER 25

How does such a disparate group of people in A.A. manage to get along so well? Research into human behavior provides us with some answers. There is the identification that takes place when a group of people under extreme danger are celebratory in being saved from the disaster. A.A. members have that feeling. Too often after the initial friendship old patterns develop and the camaraderie is lost. That can't be the reason A.A.'s maintain meaningful friendships. Researchers have found that the common bond that brought people together can be lasting if they continue to look for their commonality. Each meeting I go to I reinforce the bonds of friendship. I see myself in the other.

OCTOBER 26

Like all of our character defects, pride has two sides. There is authentic pride and false pride. Authentic pride comes from a job well done; the person has earned the rewards either physical or mental through effort. False pride is just the opposite. It rests on something a person has attributed to him by someone else or that he falsely claims is a result of his effort. I have seen bumper stickers that proclaim, "Proud to be an American", when I think it should read, "Grateful I'm an American". Most of what I am pleased about in being an American has little to do with what I have personally done. Our greatness as a nation is the result of the work over centuries of people who persevered in the face of great obstacles. I'm not proud that I belong to A.A., but I am grateful that people before me created this opportunity for sobriety. I am a grateful alcoholic.

OCTOBER 27

What makes for a successful alcoholic, one who finally gets sober and does not relapse, who practices the principles in all their affairs and who helps another alcoholic achieve sobriety? A.A.s accept the reality that their success in the long run depends on repaying the generosity of others. From the very first, men in A.A. determined that their staying sober depended on their helping another alcoholic. Where did that knowledge come from? Was it intuition? Was it a direct message from God and is tuition another name for God? In fact as noted earlier none of us can survive without the contributions of countless others. Humans live for the most part in communities based on mutual interests. Cooperation is the foundation of human society. Without help, life is impossible for any of us.

OCTOBER 28

One drunk helping another drunk is the fundamental underpinning of A.A. And all of us are grateful for the help we were given and for the help we provide others. The reciprocity of helping other is not an obligation to repay the drunks who helped us. Freely given and freely received is the assistance provided to all who want to get sober. We have no obligation to sponsor someone, to give money to A.A. , to serve the home group. And yet, most of us do that without coercion or threat of withdrawing membership in A.A. The golden rule is truly practiced in A.A. We do unto other s what we want done for us and at the same time do not really know if the still suffering alcoholic will ever do unto us what we have done for them. We want to be treated in a caring way by the alcoholic we are helping, but there is no expectation that the care will ever be reciprocated by that newcomer.

OCTOBER 29

Tolerance of others battling recognized addictions ought to be pretty easy for us alcoholics. Most of us today have no problem when telling our stories drug addiction is mentioned as long as the focus is on alcoholism. And yet I recently heard a tirade against people who are overweight riding around on those scooters taking up handicapped parking spaces. It was remarkable how much like the fulminations against alcoholism prior to the discovery of causes of our disease were to the overweight person. "They brought it on themselves. They could just stop eating so much. All they need to do is get up off their asses and do some work". The same refrains were made and with some individuals are still made about alcoholism. We may find the same problem with our brains apply to those who suffer from obesity.

OCTOBER 30

The need to belong, to be part of something other than self, drives us to leading social lives. Humans are not meant to live alone. Children raised without human touch are sorely disturbed individuals. The need for social cohesiveness is a profound human trait that has made civilization possible. That need also led me to doing what others wanted to do rather than depending on my own values of what was right and wrong. In that sense, social cohesiveness worked to my disadvantage. I did things in order to fit in and drinking, especially in my college fraternity, was a great bonding experience. The irony is that eventually my drinking would drive others away and I would be alone.

OCTOBER 31

Drinking someone under the table was considered quite an accomplishment. In a less enlightened time having a woman drink a man under the table was a sure indication that one's masculinity could be questioned. And for a woman, wow! She was one of the boys now. How much alcohol one could consume in an evening was a contest and in far too many cases turned deadly. Alcohol poisoning is a real possibility that is ignored at great peril. What kind of friend would encourage such behavior? Why would one want to engage in drinking large quantities of alcohol only to throw it up? Or shut down vital organs? Such questions do not come to one's mind when out with fellow drinkers and shows how our thinking ended by making us insane by every definition of that term.

NOVEMBER 1

One person acting alone can seldom change anything other than himself. Great numbers of people can make change happen. A.A. proves this point. Bill W. was facing great discouragement when he made the fateful call that put him in contact with Bob. It was only after attracting scores of people increasing to hundreds of people that the attitude towards alcoholism in this country underwent serious change. Prior to A.A., alcoholism was seen as a moral deficiency. Slowly and surely when scientists began to study alcoholics' behavior and do studies of the effect alcohol had on body chemistry and the mind that real understanding of alcohol has been achieved. Now we know that lots of people still deny that alcoholism is a disease and think that it is just a matter of will power, but thanks to growing amount of research that denial is being eroded.

NOVEMBER 2

Coins, chips, anniversary cakes are ways in which individuals are recognized for time passed since the last drink. Do we really need these small celebrations? We probably don't NEED them but psychologists tell us that few people continue to do what they ought to do without some sort of recognition. I belong to a YMCA fitness center that records my work on the cardio circuit and my running. It does keep me motivated as I see the pounds lifted and calories burned increase. I know that getting on the scale and seeing the weight drop is a major motivator and does just the opposite when the pounds stubbornly refuse to melt away. So, let's not deride the giving of coins and other forms of recognition. Never refuse help because of some prejudice against that help.

NOVEMBER 3

Permission to get angry? Sure. I know, I know, anger is the luxury of more balanced individuals and we alcoholics should avoid it like the plague. We can't. It's a human emotion that must have some survival value. Denial, even of anger, is not healthful. Am I suggesting that one should give in to the emotion of anger? Yes. I think that we can handle it better than we usually do. I believe that if we give ourselves three minutes to be angry and that we know quite well that we are giving ourselves the permission to be angry, it will subside. It is like: all right. Got that out of my system! Here is where the rational mind can help us as we set a time limit to the anger. This is the opposite of uncontrolled anger. It is accepting that all the human emotions are part of us and we are learning to control them rather than having them control us.

NOVEMBER 4

A major problem for me in getting sober was my intellect. I'm certifiably smart with the requisite letters after my name. I still believe in the value of education and the rational mind. While over reliance on reason can be deadly for any human, the rejection of reason and intellect is no guarantee of success in overcoming the disease of alcoholism. Relying on gut and instinct can be just as deadly and destructive in a quest for a sane and sober life. Some of us believe that our thinking got us into this trouble when just the opposite is probably true. We didn't think about the consequences and the overwhelming evidence that alcohol was not good for us. Our instinct told us that we were like other people especially those other people who seemingly drank with impunity. Relying solely on one human trait in dealing with alcohol leads inevitably to hitting bottom.

NOVEMBER 5

Moment of silence is always offered at A.A. meetings but rarely observed. What do I mean by that? Too often we are too anxious to get started or we are fearful of quiet time. The tradition of asking for a moment of silence is grounded in good theory. We need the time for setting aside all that we have had happen to us that day, the fears we have had, the disappointments we have experienced and the day to day accumulation of worries and stress. Even to set aside the successes we may have enjoyed is helpful. We need to do that so that we are open to what we are going to hear in the meeting or to listen to that small voice that is calling us for renewal. When we skip or pass too quickly to the next part of the meeting we are not allowing our God time to speak to us. If I find myself uncomfortable with silence I need to ask myself why.

NOVEMBER 6

I recently sat and listened to the guest speaker and was bothered by her apparently lack of humility. She seemed more intent on performing or entertaining us than in sharing her experience, strength and hope. She did provoke a lot of laughter and identification with a number of people at the meeting. I was reminded that every meeting does not have to meet some personal standard for the meeting to be a good one. After she quit sharing other people in the meeting told her thanks for sharing and that they could identify with her story. So, again l learned that I am not the center of the universe nor should I be the sole judge of what is helpful. I got to another meeting rather quickly and found what I needed to hear. And possibly just possibly someone at that meeting was bothered by what was said. Every meeting is a good meeting.

NOVEMBER 7

A home group supplements the knowledge and experience of one's sponsor. And the camaraderie bolsters our connectedness to others and leads us away from the isolation that was often a hallmark of our experience before coming into A.A. The danger is that the home group can become too insular forgetting the purpose of the group to help the individual stay sober and help others to achieve sobriety. It is often said that the newcomer is the most important person in the group. That may be arguable on a personal level, but for the group it is absolutely essential that we stay focused on those who are just beginning to trudge the road of happy destiny.

NOVEMBER 8

Bitterness of yesterday keeps us from the joys of the present. Bitterness is focusing on what others have done to us. Often it means overlooking one's own part in those situations that continue to haunt us if we let them. The good news of A.A. is that we can get rid of the ghosts of the past. The healing starts with an admission of one's own role in those situations. We are not absolving the others of the role they played: it does take two to tango and two to tangle. We just aren't going to let the mistakes of others dominate our thinking and our actions. That takes perseverance and time. Letting go is hard to do as expressed in our opening reading, "What an order. I can't go through with it". We can go through with it to the other side of peace within ourselves.

NOVEMBER 9

Running away is no longer an option. So many of us ran away from first wives and husbands, places of work, schools, and took geographical cures when we were active alcoholics. We acted as if the problem was outside of ourselves and that if we just changed the conditions we would be all right. Hoping that the accountability of our actions could be laid at the feet of others, we moved on to other wives, husbands, work, schools and communities finally coming to the sensible conclusion that the problem was closer to home than we wished. As mature adults today we know that we are responsible for how we react to those sometimes daunting challenges life throws at everyone. As a famous comedian once proclaimed, "the devil made me do it"! We can laugh today at such dodges from reality.

NOVEMBER 10

Acceptance can mean joyful response to the most upsetting of occurrences. Take for example a detour around a highway construction. You can curse the delay that is likely or you can look forward to seeing what you would have missed. Life is like that too. We may not travel the road we thought we were going to take, the detour may have been our alcoholism, but think of what we would have missed if we hadn't been detoured. Enjoy and accept the detours; they may lead to some unexpected pleasure.

NOVEMBER 11

I no longer feel overwhelmed by events swirling past me. I have learned patience and acceptance. When I was drinking I often complained that I couldn't get anything done, that there were too many demands on my time. What a difference sobriety makes! Taking life one day at a time means letting go of the worries of the past and worries about the future and that means focusing on what is all right at this moment. I look back to remind myself of how far I've come and I look forward to what the future holds knowing that good or bad, I will be all right.

NOVEMBER 12

So much to be thankful for and so little gratitude. I start a list of the things for which I am grateful. It begins with breathing and continues to having food on my table to sleeping safely in the comfort of my home. But gratitude is for more than physical comfort. I am at peace with my family, neighbors and friends. The small injustices remain just that, small. I live in a country where the four fundamental freedoms are alive and well. With so much hatred and vitriol dominating our public square, I remain steadfast in practicing the principles of A.A. I refuse to acquiesce to the easy despair of the current malaise knowing that this too shall pass.

NOVEMBER 13

What do we make of the inevitable storms of life? Pain has been called the chief motivator for change and I think that remains true. Storms do a lot of good in the physical world: the hurricanes that destroy also bring much needed rains while balancing the variable cold and warmth that makes this planet livable. Old trees, even ones we highly prize, may be killed but the death of the older ones makes it possible for new trees to grow. I think our personal storms are much like the weather storms. They cause damage and they may really hurt, but out of that damage come the possibility of renewal. We repair the damage where we can, replace where we must and resolve to not be caught off-guard the next time.

NOVEMBER 14

Several years ago a court ruled that A.A. was a religion and therefore people could not be coerced into attending A.A. meetings as part of rehabilitation. Better minds than mine made this decision but I do accept that I go to A.A. meetings for the same reason I attend church: for inspiration. I am inspired by the stories of how lives have been changed, how families have been reunited, how hope has been restored and how character defects have been dramatically reduced. I am moved to focus less on myself and on serving others. There is a joy in living that is heard in A.A. meetings indicating that our lives have been renewed, a joy that is very similar to what happens in churches, synagogues and mosques.

NOVEMBER 15

Listening is an attribute praised more often than it is practiced. I have been as guilty as the next person in listening at meeting preparing myself to make a contribution and therefore not really listening. My wife accuses me of preparing a rebuttal before she has made her point and I have to ruefully admit that statement has more than a kernel of truth. It is a character defect that my ego is still active when I need to have my insight, knowledge, and opinion have greater importance than those offered by another person. I must remember that I do not have to have the last word; that others offer at least as much as I do to any conversation.

NOVEMBER 16

Silver maple trees produce super abundant seedlings clogging our gutters and curbs and gardens. My neighbor thinks I should cut down the trees as she fights the same clogging of her gutters and curbs. I'm not going to cut them down, they keep the house cool in the summer without air—conditioning in addition to fighting pollution. I planted those trees over 40 years ago and if I could go back, I would plant a different species of trees. But I can't go back. The past is past. The trees are a lot like humans; we cause annoyances but we also bring goodness and we can't change our past. And like the trees I still cause problems that must be faced and cleaned up. I occasionally cross the street and sweep up the seedlings on my neighbor's property. In the words of A.A. not only do I clean up my side of the street, sometimes I am responsible for cleaning up both sides

BILL E.

NOVEMBER 17

A friend of mine got sober shortly after I did and has not taken a drink of alcohol in the intervening years. He attended a few A.A. meetings but has not attended a meeting for quite some time. He is sober, but he hasn't had a personality change. He still argues, sometimes quite loudly with his wife and still demands that family members do what he wants done. Quitting drinking is easy, following the suggested program of A.A. is difficult and requires constant vigilance that can best be achieved by a daily reminder of what it was like and what it is like now. Old patterns of behavior will resurface even for those of us who continue to work the Steps.

NOVEMBER 18

If we are to succeed, we must engage in lifelong learning. The skills, knowledge and attitude of what we learned in high school or college will not suffice. Oh, a large part of me resists this reality of our modern life. Our knowledge is doubling at a terrific rate and the machines we use are being upgraded continually. I want the quiet comfort of the known and yet I cannot avoid the rapid changes occurring at a breathtaking speed. With all the changes though, some things remain true and unchallenged. Our emotional lives and needs have not changed in thousands of years. No matter how much the physical world changes we need love and acceptance and a sense of security. Our drinking cut us off from those basic needs.

NOVEMBER 19

America's story emphasizes how differing tribes of people came here and learned to get past the differences that caused such grief in the Old Country. E pluribus Unum, one out of many, is a powerful image that challenges us to live up to our aspiration. Our country is remarkable even though the history has been blemished by our failure to live up to this ideal. A.A. represents the best of that ideal. Diverse people who would normally not associate with each other come together in common cause of living alcohol free. The common bond remarkably is not bondage: we are bound together in love not in repression.

NOVEMBER 20

We gossip, we curse when things don't go our way, we procrastinate and we avoid making hard decisions. And yet, somehow, we also manage to praise others for their success, we take action and we make those difficult choices. In other words we are human. What remains remarkable is the good we do is greater than the harm we do. That is often the reversal of our behavior when we were drinking. Of course we remain self-centered and our egos get bruised and we strike out in anger. That is when we work the 10th Step and admit to ourselves and others how we fell short of the ideal. We are all too human and that includes the human characteristic of making amends.

NOVEMBER 21

Acceptance is from the root word accept which the dictionary defines as to receive willingly and to regard as proper and true. We do not always like to hear or be reminded of what is true and proper. We sometimes cling stubbornly to beliefs just because we have held them for a long time or because it means admitting that some other person has been more correct than we have been. The old character defect of envy is always close to the surface. And so with reluctance we accede to what is manifestly true and we quit fighting. Being willing is not always an easy attribute to demonstrate.

NOVEMBER 22

There are two words that have profound importance for recovering alcoholics: humility and responsibility. The first requires an admission that a power greater than ourselves, alcohol, has taken control of our lives and that we need help if we are recover any control over our lives. The second term, responsibility, means that because of the help we have received, we can no longer blame anyone else for what happened and will happen to us. Humility also means that whatever success we have, it is incumbent upon us to acknowledge that we are not solely responsible for that success.

NOVEMBER 23

We owe God an amend or two, maybe even more. We were given great intelligence and didn't use it to an advantage; we were given good health and didn't take care of our body; we were given conscience and failed to be compassionate. When we allowed alcohol to dominate our lives, we failed in school or didn't live up to the possibilities; we harmed our hearts, lives and kidneys with excessive alcohol intake; we were self-centered and ignored the help we could have given others. When making a list of all persons we have harmed, we do need to apologize to our Creator and to take action to use our abilities in the way that our Creator intended.

NOVEMBER 24

Into every life a little rain must fall. What strange people we are who see rain as something we must endure instead of welcoming it as essential to life on this planet. Thank goodness for rain. And thank goodness for the pain we must endure, for without pain we would surely die. Pain tells us that something is wrong—we are hurting either physically or emotionally. It was pain that finally brought me to a program of recovery. And just as there can be too much rain at any given time resulting in floods, so too can pain be too much. We try to prepare for the floods by building retaining walls. We prepare for the pain that is inevitable by having a spiritual wall.

NOVEMBER 25

I suppose that all of us at one time or another each of us has asked the question, "What is the meaning of life?" Part of the answer is really rather simple: to participate consciously in the most mundane of human activities. We may be doing the newcomer a disservice when we claim that what will happen will be "beyond your wildest dreams." Most of us spent our drinking years chasing excitement when the reality is that life cannot be peak experience after peak experience. Taking care of our family, spending time with the sick and elderly, washing the car and preparing meals are examples of the mundane activities that in the end give meaning to our existence. Now that may count as a wild dream, but I don't think that will sell with the newcomer.

NOVEMBER 26

Ben Franklin wrote, "He that teaches himself has a fool for his master". So it is with us when we tried to get sober on our own. Countless attempts at the next time will be different to all the ways of trying to reduce the dependency on alcohol from trying to limit the drinks per hour, to changing the type of liquor consumed was met with failure. We did not know that we were in the grips of a disease that could not be conquered by self will alone. That lack of knowledge was abetted by a culture that saw alcoholism as a moral failing. We had a fool as a master.

NOVEMBER 27

It's not easy being a sponsor. We can and do give advice and suggestions but we cannot give conduct. The naïve belief on my part that by superior logic and example, I believed I could successfully lead others to follow the simple Steps of A.A. I was disabused of that idea with the very first person I sponsored. Humility is one of the gifts of sponsoring others. I soon learned that the results I was experiencing were matched by others in the program. We cannot get others sober—that is a job for the individual and his Higher Power. In 1935 there was widespread belief that very little could be done for the alcoholic. Today we know that very much can be done, if the flesh and spirit are willing.

NOVEMBER 28

Our automobiles and our behavior are often mentioned in A.A. meetings. Most of us state that we often let our patience and humility go out the window while driving. I think the problem is that our ego is involved when we are driving as it is less involved in other aspects of our lives. There is something about the anonymity of the car that is our downfall. If we could only remember that the person driving too slowly or too quickly or meandering over the road, or any other aspect of their driving may be having a bad day. Our ego says that they are trying to dominate us and that may be the furthest thing from the truth.

NOVEMBER 29

Why do I have such difficulty in remembering names of people I meet in A.A.? Of course it is not just in A.A. meetings that I have that difficulty. For me at least the reason is simple. I think it is because I am more interested in impressing the individual than in really paying attention to the person or their name. It means of course that I am possessed of a strong ego and that I am focused too much on self. There are lots of good recommendations on remembering names that it would do me good to follow. Here is a case of knowing and not doing that indicates knowledge alone is not enough.

NOVEMBER 30

Who makes the better teacher? The one who got all A's in the subject matter he is teaching, or the one who struggled, got some C's and B' and the occasional A? Surprisingly, it is the latter student that often makes the better teacher. That seems to defy common sense. But there is substantial evidence to say common sense doesn't work here. The latter teacher knows where the difficulty comes in learning the subject. He can help students when they are struggling. It is the same principle of one alcoholic helping another alcoholic. One who has struggled with alcohol knows the pitfalls and difficulties that the non-alcoholic often doesn't understand.

DECEMBER 1

How can one do God's work in the beginning stages of recovery? The same way the long-timer can do God's work. She can smile which is a simple thing. We alcoholics know that we complicate some of the simplest things. The founders of A.A. spoke of this as a danger to the recovering alcoholic. God's work sounds so important, complicated and best left to those with a better grounding in spiritual matters. It doesn't have to be. In addition to smiling and giving a feeling of welcome is one of those ways, but includes attending meetings, driving someone to a meeting, setting up the meeting room. When we do it for the least of these, we do it for our higher power.

DECEMBER 2

"My friends got me drunk last night." It is a familiar refrain that ignores the reality that no one can get another one drunk. It is a one person job. But those who continue to believe such nonsense are either in the beginning stages of alcoholism or in that familiar place of denial. We can also question whether the people who encouraged us to get drunk are in fact friends. It is a strange definition of friendship when the friend encourages unhealthy behavior. When we say we are responsible, we lay claim to adulthood.

DECEMBER 3

"All the world's a stage and men and women mere actors." This from one of Shakespeare's great plays is appropriate for us recovering alcoholics. When we recount the episodes of our time while drinking, we are remembering the acts we took in trying to cover our feelings of inferiority. Alcohol gave us the courage to do what we would not normally have done without the aid of booze. We really didn't know who we were especially if we began drinking at an early age. We did not find out who we were because we were acting as we imagined we ought to act. With sobriety we had to learn a new script, one based on a realistic assessment of our strength and weaknesses.

DECEMBER 4

George Burns's song, "I wish I were 18 again, going where I'd never been" could be an A.A. song. Not that many of us would want to be 18 again, but the time we first took steps to recovery has its appeal. The wonder we had when we realized we had awakened instead of coming to in the morning; when we knew what we had done the night before; when we first felt the relief that came from the Fourth and Fifth Steps; when we felt a burden lifted when we made our amends; when we gained a sense of worth when we helped our first sponsee. All of these await the newcomer and so in one sense of the word we envy them for the discoveries that lie ahead. None of us want to return to the feelings of helplessness when we first came to A.A. But the joy that began to happen for the first time is priceless.

DECEMBER 5

As a teacher I know that the person who comes to class will do better than the student who doesn't. The student who comes to class and reads the book will do better than the student who doesn't. The student who comes to class, reads the book and underlines what he has read will do better that the student who doesn't. The student, who comes to class, reads the book, underlines what he has read and talks to other students about what he has learned will do better than the student who doesn't. And finally the student who does all those things and then teaches it to another student will do better than the student who doesn't. The same can be said for those of us in A. A. The more we are engaged the more likely will we learn what we need to learn. We also know that repetition is almost always necessary to be good at something. Practice does not make perfect, it makes permanent.

DECEMBER 6

When I say I loved beer and liquor I mean it almost literally. Think of someone you truly love and what do you do? You spend an inordinate amount of time with that person, and when you are not with him or her you think of that individual almost constantly, you spend a lot of money on that person, and you feel as if life wouldn't we worth living if you had to give her or him up. Doesn't that describe our relationship with booze? That may explain why most of us feel restless and irritable the first few days of sobriety and it explains why so many go back to drinking. Booze was more than a friend even when the "friend" was bad for us.

DECEMBER 7

Growing up on a farm we practiced crop rotation where every three years one of the fields would lie fallow; that is no food crops only grass would be planted. That period of rest was important for sustaining the land. So, too do we need to lie fallow some of the time in A.A. Even in working the Steps of the program we do ourselves no good if we don't take it easy every so often. Meditation is also a form of lying fallow, to slow down and rest and prepare for the work ahead. The saying, "All work and no play makes Jack a dull boy", applies to recovering alcoholics. Enjoy the fruits of your labor in getting sober and then return refreshed to the task of maintaining sobriety.

DECEMBER 8

When we applaud the person celebrating an anniversary, we are not just celebrating one person's accomplishment: we are really celebrating our program of recovery. We do not get sober on our own; we need the help of others. So, the applause is for the individual for sure, but also for the men and women who were there when we came into the rooms, who encouraged us, who challenged us, who were doing what they needed to do to stay sober. We also recognize that effort that is not acknowledged will diminish over time and so we celebrate the individual and A.A.

DECEMBER 9

One on one learning with a master teacher and an apprentice has a long record of success. People learn best from contact with a person who is good at what he is doing. Crucial to the teacher and the student is that there has to be a high tolerance for ambiguity and for making mistakes. We try something and we fail at it we have two choices: to analyze what caused the mistake or to throw up our hands and quit. How many people come into A.A. find the tasks difficult, have a slip and quit? Far more than those who slip and then talk over the reason for their failure with a master also known as a sponsor. And while we may not slip we do fail to do what we know we ought to do. As a long time member I still need to analyze why the character defects keep reoccurring.

DECEMBER 10

The most insidious lie that we tell ourselves is that a drink will make it better. If we have had a rough day at the office, or if the kids at home have been especially trying, or if we lost a ballgame or for that matter any negative experience can be made better with an alcoholic drink. When we are reminded in A.A. meetings that in fact nothing will be made better with a drink that in fact alcohol will make things worse, it doesn't ring true. Newcomers question that value and only come to appreciate the reality that alcohol has no redeeming quality in making things better over a period of time. What it does do is delay facing the negative situation.

DECEMBER 11

"The sun will come out tomorrow", a line from a famous play and movie is a good motto for alcoholics. It is a close cousin to the statement, "this too shall pass". The world will little note nor long remember what you are experiencing. Even when there is a national calamity and it seems that all the citizens are glued to their TV sets, most of life for most of the people continue interrupted only temporarily. There is always other news other than the major story. So, it is with us and our personal narrative. Life will go on, the sun will rise in the east, this sadness will pass and you will accept that which you cannot change.

DECEMBER 12

Living without fear is not possible. It is a human emotion that our ancestors needed in order to survive a hostile environment. There were saber-toothed tigers and vicious snakes that could bring death. These were healthy fears. They encouraged caution and paying attention to surroundings. We recognize our healthy fears—that the advertising come-ons are tempting, a friendly round of golf may end at the 19th hole, a toast at a wedding, all can lead to dire consequences for us. We need to pay attention to our surroundings—they contain dangers that are as real as those tigers were for our forebears.

DECEMBER 13

Sometimes we are stuck and cannot move. We are like the car caught in a mud hole—all the rocking back and forth and spinning of tires brings us no closer to release from the mud hole. We eventually call for help. We don't just sit there hoping that the car will miraculously free its self. In sobriety we can become stuck—unable apparently to move to the next step and so we call on our sponsor or on our higher power or on both. It is in this admission of powerlessness that we can move on with our sober lives. When we say we can't do what is asked of us in A.A. we are admitting that we need help in freeing ourselves from the hole we are in.

DECEMBER 14

There is a great appeal in the advertising slogan, "What happens in Vegas stays in Vegas". No matter what outrageous behavior you engage in will not lead to any negative consequences. That's a powerful promise giving the individual an assurance that whatever he did would have no long range affect on his life. We often acted as if that slogan was the basis of our life. After a night of too much revelry we hoped and prayed that whatever we did and couldn't remember would be ignored by those we cared about. At some point what we did caused us such pain we finally had to admit that what happened to us did stay with us.

DECEMBER 15

Resiliency is a powerful human trait that serves the individual well. Individuals who learn how to deal with changes in life do better than those who won't or can't. The loss of a marriage, job or house can be grieved, but these events are common. An ability or willingness to accept and adapt to the new situation is the hallmark of a healthy individual. That ability plays a key role in getting and staying sober. It has been said that a broken shoestring has caused more relapses than any other cause. That may be an exaggeration but illustrates a fundamental truth: stuff happens and accepting and adapting to the change leads to continued sobriety.

DECEMBER 16

How to eat nutritionally consists of well-known and rather easily followed instructions for most of us. We know that serving size, number of calories in the meal, how many vitamins, minerals, fat, cholesterol and sodium are in the foods we eat. They are printed on the food we buy and the recipes we follow. Just because this information is readily available doesn't mean that we will pay attention to that information. So, it is with our program of sobriety. We know what we need to do. Knowing is not enough. Action has to take place.

DECEMBER 17

Many of us have had dreams fulfilled. There are also an equal number if not greater, whose lives are only better with the ending of the chaos that we created when drinking. I think we do harm to the newcomer when we assert that their lives now are going to somehow be spectacular. It is better to promise little but deliver a lot than to do the opposite. It should be good enough that are lives are returned to some level of normality. Sitting on the bar stool promising ourselves that tomorrow we were going to conquer the world wasn't realistic then and isn't any more realistic now that we are sober.

DECEMBER 18

We used to love the chaos that often surrounded our drinking. The excitement of being with people who were on the edge of performing in a disturbing manner often proved irresistible. And then the pleasure of being able to recite what had happened and to be part of the story telling about the behavior the next day made us feel a part of something bigger than ourselves. Unless, and this was a big unless, we had been the one that had been the center of that performance. Craving that type of excitement is gone. So is the embarrassment that accompanied our behavior.

DECEMBER 19

When to walk away from an unpleasant situation is one of the benefits of getting sober. The physical and emotional scars that resulted from too many scrapes with other unsavory characters often led us to declare, "No more" only to be back in the same or similar situation the next day. Today we do not have to prove our physical or mental superiority especially in those situations where the other person is under the influence. We can simply take a few breaths breathing deeply and repeat the Serenity Prayer. We have nothing to prove knowing that our sobriety is more important than winning any argument.

DECEMBER 20

Rome wasn't built in a day and neither will your sober life be built in a day. As with any construction you can expect delays, set-backs, and time when nothing seems to be getting done. A good foundation requires patience and care because if you try to rush the job inevitably something goes wrong. Every item used in construction may not be available when needed; your sponsor may not be able to respond to your immediate needs. Meditation is recommended as a practice for recovering alcoholics and that requires taking time out and is essential in building a sober life. Remember patience is a virtue even in recovery.

DECEMBER 21

Like life itself, the game of chess requires great concentration, planning ahead and the ability to make the right moves. The game has proven to develop these skills especially in those kids for whom little else in life has given them those characteristics. The game of a sober life requires the same abilities that will come with working the Twelve Steps. And like chess, few of us will become masters of the game often losing concentration, failing to plan ahead and not often enough making the right moves. It is all right as long as we accept progress rather than perfection.

DECEMBER 22

The bathroom mirror told us more about our drinking excesses than any words from friends. The bleary eyes, the sunken cheeks and the tousled hair was a warning that could be avoided until we stepped in front of the mirror and the consequences of too much drinking for too long a period of time could no longer be intellectually denied. Too many of us continued denying what booze was doing to us even though the evidence kept piling up. The mirror didn't lie and we eventually had to accept as truth what the mirror had been telling us: booze was doing us in.

DECEMBER 23

Admitting to our character defects has been likened to peeling an onion. Think of the onion as a look at the complete set of character defects. Layer after layer is pulled away often causing much tears and regrets for our past behavior. It is not pleasant nor is it meant to be. We cannot begin to change until we know what we need to change. That is why just saying you're sorry after a particular nasty episode is not enough. Getting through the layers of unbecoming conduct and thoughts makes it possible to move toward the person you want to be.

DECEMBER 24

The human body goes through periods of great growth both physically and mentally. All of us are familiar with the body growth associated with adolescence but there have been similar growth spurts all along the years. With the spurts have been long periods of time when nothing seems to be changing on an outward basis. The same can be said about our recovery when we seem to get stuck. But like the human body unseen changes preparing for the growth periods are occurring. Just because we cannot see them doesn't mean they are not happening. It is when the excitement of change seems to bog down that our recovery is in danger. Patience is required. Changes are occurring for the next stage of growth.

DECEMBER 25

The well-known Christmas carol, "Silent Night, Holy Night" has special appeal to alcoholics. In recovery our nights are now silent and all is calm compared to the nights when we came home from heavy drinking causing noise and commotion and turmoil. How much better this is not only for those we love but for ourselves. What kind of life would it be if we lived in constant sunlight without the coolness of the evening and the reflection that darkness can bring us? May our nights remain silent and holy.

DECEMBER 26

My oldest son and I were engaged in emailing comments back and forth to one another and I made a disparaging remark about a businessman widely known to the public. He wrote back that I was being too harsh on the man and that he could also be judged by the good he had done. I responded with a "you're right and I'm wrong". His response was illuminating when he asked if I were serious in the admission or did I just not want to argue. Apparently he wasn't used to me so easily admitting that I was wrong. It takes a long time to convince people we have changed.

DECEMBER 27

Our feelings do not last. One of our wedding gifts was a trivet that said, "Kissing don't last, cookery do". How true that is. In the initial stages of Eros we are sure that our feelings towards the person will last. They do and they don't. They change and then the hard work of marriage begins as we begin the daily routines necessary for survival including cooking. The same can be said for sobriety. The initial stage has been described as pink cloud where everything seems oh so grand. And then the reality of everyday living with all of its work and lack of excitement intrudes and we begin the hard work of staying sober.

DECEMBER 28

A.A. is a spiritual program, not a religious one. Spirituality is a difficult term to get our hearts and minds around. We have a "spirited defense" of an idea. We have our "spirits" uplifted by a winning touchdown. And we call most alcoholic beverages "spirits". The commonality in all of these is that they make us feel good from the experiences. That is one reason why alcohol has such a powerful pull. For us in A.A. spirituality can be viewed as that feeling we get for doing good, the good we do when we help another alcoholic recover. Spiritual people are recognized for their unselfishness in providing that help.

DECEMBER 29

In observing other people's drinking habits two things happen when we quit drinking. We are surprised that most people do not care if we are drinking or not and the most surprising discovery is that great numbers of people do not slug down their drinks but sip their drinks. In early recovery I was startled and somewhat disturbed that my wife could nurse a drink for long periods of time. Those who nurse their drinks do not like the feeling of the effects of alcohol. Not so with us. Feeling the effects of alcohol was why we wanted to drink. Non-alcoholics do not like that feeling.

DECEMBER 30

In Upstate New York we had an unusually snowless beginning of winter so when the snow did come in great abundance we felt reassured that all was right with the world. We like the rhythm of the seasons in this part of the country and even though we may eventually become discouraged with the snow, we know that this too shall pass. So it is with our lives. When we get sober there is something comforting in the normal events of our lives. Good things are more likely to happen in normal circumstances than in disturbing circumstances.

DECEMBER 31

Many of our local meetings include not only coffee but cookies. Our culture includes food at almost every type of event and A.A. is not different in this respect. I have found myself on more than a few occasions noting that my liking of cookies is reminiscent of my drinking. I start with one or two promising myself that I will only take those two. Yet far too often I keep picking just one more. My drinking was often like that: I didn't need the drink nor did I really want it but since it was there well I might as well enjoy it. Cookies are different than my similar reactions with alcohol because I can continue to enjoy them without terrible results for me or others.

Made in the USA
Lexington, KY
03 August 2015